T0243447

"Neil Seeman courageously examines the excesses of forms of entrepreneurialism unmoored from historic conceptions of innovation for the greater good. He is the first to explain how entrepreneurs, artists, and risk-takers of all types can better manage the successive bursts of dopamine swooshing in their brains."
– Lord Anthony St John, Crossbench Member of the House of Lords

"This timely book amalgamates an autobiography, frank descriptions of mission-driven or profit-driven entrepreneurs, their anguished personal and professional risks, with conceivable underlying biological drivers."
– Bertha K. Madras, PhD, professor of psychobiology,
Harvard Medical School

"Combining scholarly analysis with dramatic personal history, Neil Seeman clearly frames the mental challenges entrepreneurs face, and offers hope for the future. A real dopamine rush."
– Myles Druckman, MD, senior vice president and
global medical director, International SOS

"*Accelerated Minds* is a tour de force. Seeman offers no less than a treatise on entrepreneurship, a primer on dopamine in neuromodulation, and a touch of philosophy—and he makes it all gel elegantly."
– Frederick Lowy, OC, MD, FRCP, former dean of medicine,
University of Toronto, and former president and
vice-chancellor of Concordia University

ACCELERATED MINDS

Dedicated, with love, to my parents,
Mary and Philip Seeman.

Written, with gratitude, for the quiet
entrepreneurs among us.

ACCELERATED MINDS

UNLOCKING THE FASCINATING, INSPIRING, AND OFTEN DESTRUCTIVE IMPULSES THAT DRIVE THE ENTREPRENEURIAL BRAIN

BY NEIL SEEMAN

SUTHERLAND HOUSE

TORONTO, 2023

Sutherland House
416 Moore Ave., Suite 205
Toronto, ON M4G 1C9

First edition, Spring 2023

If you are interested in inviting one of our authors to a live event or
media appearance, please contact sranasinghe@sutherlandhousebooks.com
and visit our website at sutherlandhousebooks.com for more
information about our authors and their schedules.

We acknowledge the support of the Government of Canada.

Manufactured in India
Cover designed by Lena Yang
Book composed by Karl Hunt

Library and Archives Canada Cataloguing in Publication
Title: Accelerated minds : unlocking the fascinating, inspiring, and often
destructive impulses that drive the entrepreneurial brain / Neil Seeman.
Names: Seeman, Neil, author.
Description: Includes index.
Identifiers: Canadiana (print) 20220482144 | Canadiana (ebook) 20220482187 |
ISBN 9781990823046 (hardcover) | ISBN 9781990823206 (EPUB)
Subjects: LCSH: Entrepreneurship—Psychological aspects. |
LCSH: Risk-taking (Psychology) | LCSH: Brain.
Classification: LCC HB615 .S417 2023 |
DDC 338/.04—dc23

ISBN 978-1-990823-04-6
eBook 978-1-990823-20-6

CONTENTS

1

THE CRISIS IN ENTREPRENEURSHIP

ARON SWARTZ HANGED HIMSELF in January 2013 at the age of twenty-six. He was an acknowledged Internet genius since the age of fourteen when he co-authored RSS (Really Simple Syndication), the standard that allows for easy distribution of and subscription to content that is published online.

Already at that early age, Swartz had an idealistic mission—information on the Internet needed to be free for everyone—and he had the technological skills to make that happen. In 2001, he had co-created the Creative Commons, the now ubiquitous licensing architecture that allows the sharing of knowledge openly on the Internet. It is thanks to this work that we can access academic scholarship that was once hidden behind paywalls and institutional guardrails.

In 2005, as a student at Stanford, Swartz started Infogami, an Internet archive portal. Infogami merged with Reddit, a democratic social news aggregation, content-rating, and discussion website. Reddit reshaped our understanding of what interaction on the Internet could feel like. Although it's familiar to us now, when it was first introduced, Reddit had an aura of magic about it, giving people the power to talk to each other about any topic at any moment and interact with anyone who was willing to sign up for a Reddit AMA (short for "Ask Me Anything"). All you needed was a computer and an Internet connection and with a bit of luck you were in conversation with the likes of billionaire philanthropist Bill Gates or Peter Moore, the longest-held hostage in Iraq. In its early days, Reddit was the realization of a particular ideal of what we always imagined the Internet could be: free information, elegantly organized from the bottom up rather than the top down, the very opposite of traditional 1980s media.

Like most entrepreneurs I know, Swartz was not in it solely or even primarily to make money. He was far more interested in the impact he could make on the world—what Apple co-founder Steve Jobs called making "a dent in the universe"—than in material rewards.[1] His specific passion was for creating and disseminating knowledge. In 2008, Swartz released his Guerilla Open Access

---

1 Jobs' widow, philanthropist Laurene Powell Jobs, felt she needed to explain what her late husband meant by the word "dent" in an interview she gave to *The New York Times* in 2020. To make a "dent" requires the entrepreneur to be able to manipulate circumstances, she said, or look "at the design of the structures and systems that govern our society and [change] those structures."

Manifesto, which explains his ideology of freedom of access to cultural and scientific resources. Information is power, he wrote, and information must not be siloed or locked away in an Ivy League library. Everyone should have access to the world's scientific and cultural heritage. It was his belief in opening up scientific databases to the world, his support for and engagement in Internet piracy, that got him into trouble with private publishing houses and indicted on several felony charges for illegal downloading.

Why would this brilliant young man, whose building blocks of computing innovation continue to provide new knowledge and insight into a wide variety of important topics around the world, want to end his life? He seemed to be *full* of life. He was over-energetic, bristling with ambitious and idealistic goals, always the contrarian, never afraid to flout social norms. We know there were external circumstances—there always are—but his legal challenges don't explain much. On January 10, 2013, Swartz' partner described him as replete with energy, animated, talkative, hungry. The very next day, he would not get out of bed. That evening, she came home and found him hanging from a belt in his Brooklyn apartment. That sudden switch of mood had been seen in Swartz before by close friends—what did it mean?

For all his dedication to openness, Swartz did not tell the world much about himself. He kept his most troubling piece of knowledge—that he struggled with depression—to himself. Many entrepreneurs do this, as if a mental health vulnerability were a scarlet letter of weakness, something that would stamp you and follow you, exposing you as unable to control yourself, let alone the universe that you seek to dent.

Anthony Bourdain is a familiar name to anyone who loves food or watches television. He was an author and celebrity chef who travelled the world documenting cultures and cuisines. His CNN show, *Parts Unknown*, debuted in 2013 and ran for 103 one-hour episodes over twelve seasons. It won five Emmy awards. "Bourdain broke bread with people from all walks of life—from heads of state to Syrian refugees—with meals serving as a grand equalizer," said *People* magazine.

While most think of him as a television performer, Anthony Bourdain was a man of many parts: a talented chef and successful author deeply engaged with the world around him. He was known for his antiwar stories, his respect for all cultures and socio-economic classes, and his environmental concerns. He believed that storytelling had the power to build new bonds among communities. He was also very much an entrepreneur, running ambitious restaurants, developing and producing an impressive series of television programs and movies, and launching his own publishing imprint with Ecco Press. On June 8, 2018, at the height of his popularity, the sixty-one-year-old Bourdain was found hanging in his hotel room in Strasbourg, France.

Again, there were circumstances. Bourdain wrote openly about his experiences with cocaine, heroin, LSD, and alcohol. His romantic life was complicated and, at the time, difficult. He was susceptible to depression and suicidal impulses. The label "Hemingway of gastronomy" attached to him for his mood swings as well as his writing. What caused the mood swings? Was it something foreordained, built into his DNA? Was it the pressures of the life he lived and the hurts and disappointments he encountered? Was he especially sensitive to the injustices he saw in the world? And, if so, what accounted for his sensitivity?

It is well known that more men than women end their own lives, even though depression is reported to be twice as frequent in women as it is in men, a paradox that has long perplexed mental health experts. Women do, however, also take their lives. Three days before Bourdain died, an entrepreneur known the world over, Kate Spade, committed suicide in her Manhattan apartment at age fifty-five.

Kate Spade was a fashion trailblazer and role model for many American women. While working at *Mademoiselle* magazine, she had noted a lack of affordable, stylish handbags for women. She began designing prototypes with Scotch Tape and paper. Her first proper model, "The Sam," was functional, sophisticated looking, and priced within reach of Manhattan's young working women. It was a hit in 1993, the same year her eponymous company (her husband's name, not hers) was founded. Three years later, she opened her first boutique in SoHo. Three years after that, she brought in the Neiman Marcus Group as a partner and her handbags soon hung on shelves, shoulders, and shopping trolleys around the world.

From the outside, Kate Spade appeared to have it all. Married to her business partner, Andy, they had a daughter in 2005. Her business continued to expand and in 2017 she was inducted to the Entrepreneur Hall of Fame and named "one of the most creative people in business."

With Kate Spade's suicide, again, there were external circumstances. Ten months prior to her suicide by hanging, Spade and her husband separated. But Andy Spade reported that he'd spoken to her the night before she took her life and she'd sounded happy—that could mean she had made her decision. Andy Spade shared with the world that Kate had been struggling with depression and anxiety for years. She had apparently seen doctors and taken medications.

On the other hand, her sister said that Kate Spade resisted seeking the serious medical attention that she evidently needed. As a woman in a mostly men's business world, did she worry about appearing weak, incapable of summoning the power to manipulate circumstances to her own needs? These days, many high school and college girls speak openly about being on antidepressants; it seems almost routine for young women to discuss their decisions to seek therapy in public forums. But speaking out about feeling depressed when you are an entrepreneur is rare for both women and men.

Advising *others* about emotions came easily to serial entrepreneur Tony Hsieh. He launched a not terribly successful earthworm breeding business at the age of nine, then became famous in 1999 at the age of twenty-four when he sold LinkExchange, a company he founded, to Microsoft for $265 million. He was a hero to many in the nascent ad tech community of the time. LinkExchange was innovative in its simplicity, knitting together a cooperative of websites into one thematic focus and making a lot of money while doing so.

After selling LinkExchange, Hsieh and his business partner, Alfred Lin, founded the Internet incubator Venture Frogs. Among the companies they invested in were OpenTable, Ask Jeeves, and Zappos, the online shoe retailer. Hsieh eventually served as CEO of Zappos, vaulting its sales from $1.6 million to over $1 billion annually.

Ever the idealist, Hsieh used the proceeds from his commercial endeavours to launch utopian communities. One was a collection of thirty Airstream trailers and miniature houses in an abandoned Las Vegas parking lot, where Hsieh lived for a time with two alpacas. He also bought a string of residential properties in the resort town of Park City, Utah, where he threw huge parties that seldom ended before he had wowed everyone with his flamethrower. This was a device that shot fireballs up to twenty-five feet in the air every few seconds, a metaphor, perhaps, for his high-flying ambition.

Unfailingly generous to friends and employees, he offered to double the salaries of employees who moved with him to Park City. In his 2010 bestselling book, *Delivering Happiness: A Path to Profits, Passion, and Purpose,* Hsieh laid out the values to which many of us in the entrepreneurial community aspire. With a clear sense of unwavering purpose, he argued, we are capable of taking charge not only of events around us but also of our own emotions and impulses. We are not slaves, he said, to our early programming. We have the capacity to reprogram ourselves, sweep obstacles from our path, and achieve calm and contentment. He emphasized the importance of playfulness and egalitarianism in the workplace. Corporations paid handsomely for his secret-key-to-happiness lectures.

Tony Hsieh's brain ran too fast. According to *Forbes* magazine, a friend wrote to him shortly before his death saying, in part, "I need to tell you that I don't think you are well and in your right mind . . . I think you are taking too many drugs . . ." On November 27, 2020,

Hsieh died from smoke inhalation. He had barricaded himself in a shed next to a friend's home after a quarrel. The shed caught fire from a number of potentially intentional causes, according to firefighters. "Had he set the fires himself?" some wondered.

In *Happy at Any Cost, The Revolutionary Vision and Fatal Quest of Zappos CEO Tony Hsieh*, co-authors Kirsten Grind and Katherine Sayre write that, despite the outward appearance of a workplace-happiness guru—Hsieh was privately in pain. He reportedly suffered from face blindness (prosopagnosia), a condition that made it hard for him to recognize anyone, even close friends. Oliver Sacks, the British neurologist, apparently also suffered from this condition. The authors mention that Hsieh was on the autism spectrum, depressive, and that he abused not only alcohol but nitrous oxide, or "laughing gas." Nitrous oxide is popular at raves and music festivals. It isn't as fatal as many other recreational or illicit drugs, but nor is it harmless, especially inside a burning, barricaded shed. Hsieh's may not have been a typical suicide attempt. Hsieh was a big-time gambler and risk taker. His final act may have been a challenge to his friends: "Win or lose, will you save me in time?" He had apparently asked them to check on him every five to ten minutes in the shed. They came too late.

Swartz, Bourdain, Spade, and Hsieh are high-profile names in the entrepreneurial community, but contributions to the entrepreneurial suicide rate come from lower-profile members as well.

Jody Sherman, the Las Vegas founder of Ecomom, a baby product company, shot himself in 2013 at age forty-seven. Ilya Zhitomirskiy, age twenty-two, software developer and founder of the Diaspora social network—"a project of pure passion," he told *New York* magazine—killed himself by helium asphyxiation in 2011.

Austen Heinz, age thirty-one, founder and CEO of Cambrian Genomics, took his own life in May 2015. One iconic Silicon Valley–based investor and entrepreneur told me that Heinz, a dedicated surfer who had attended Duke on an ROTC scholarship, was "the biggest surprise to all of us. He was a cool kid. Are the cool kids really the ones who commit suicide? When does *that* happen?" Mental health professionals unfortunately know that "cool" on the outside is not a good indicator of what goes on inside.

Entrepreneur suicide is not just a North American phenomenon. Adolf Merckle, born in the Sudetenland, occupied by Hitler's armies in 1938 when Merckle was four years old, became the founder of a major generic drug company, Ratiopharm, and the fifth richest person in Germany. In 2009, he threw himself under a speeding train, leaving a wife and four children.

Peter Claessens, an agricultural entrepreneur and one of the richest people in Hungary, killed himself in July 2022 at the age of forty-seven. He and his family came from Belgium. In 1995, they bought a long unwanted and neglected farm and created an ultramodern livestock company, which grew to encompass ten operating sites. In June 2022, a month before his death, Claessens was awarded the Hungarian Order of Merit from the country's Ministry of Foreign Affairs and Trade.

New Zealand entrepreneur and risk taker, Jake Millar, who founded the multi-billion-dollar companies Unfiltered and Oompher when still in his teens, hung himself in 2021 from a balcony in Kenya at the age of twenty-six.

Chinese entrepreneur Kankan Mao, who dropped out of school to start his own digital gaming firm, MaJoy, ended his life by gas inhalation at the age of thirty-five. He had been an entrepreneurial idol for Chinese youth, working on mobile health care and traffic information apps. The very definition of a serial entrepreneur, he was also involved in electronic sports. "Every entrepreneur is a hero, no matter whether he is successful," he wrote in his autobiography. In 2018, he succumbed to depression and committed suicide.

In each of these stories, there were external pressures: Merckle fared poorly in the 2008–2009 financial crisis; Claessens had been accused of tax fraud; Millar had been in the middle of what he called a "media tsunami"; Mao had failed to raise sufficient funds for his many businesses.

The suicide rate of entrepreneurs in India—said to be one an hour—is especially alarming. In 2012, a Mumbai entrepreneur, Lalit Sheth, owner of Raj Travels, died by jumping off a bridge into the sea. He left a suicide note in the car where his chauffeur was awaiting his return. In 2017, Ram Khiladi from New Delhi, aged forty-five, shot himself after his furniture company crumbled. He apparently suffered from ongoing depression. Sajan Parayil, forty-nine, hanged himself at his house in June 2019. This was after the construction of his state-of-the-art convention centre in Kerala was stalled by the civic authority. A depressed Delhi businessman, Madhur Malani, forty-four years old, killed his children, aged six and fourteen, before jumping in front of a subway train. His business, a sandpaper factory, had been shuttered and he was unemployed. The death in 2020 of award-winning Indian industrialist Joy Arakkal, managing director of the Innova Group of Companies based in

Dubai, shocked those who knew him. He had jumped from the fourteenth floor of a building, reportedly desperate over financial setbacks.

These are just a few of an abundance of similar stories. Collectively, they beg disturbing questions. Why do so many entrepreneurs succumb to addictions, anxieties, depressions, suicidal thoughts, and other temptations, such as taking advantage of people they initially set out to aid? Why do so many entrepreneurs and super creatives take excessive financial risks and put themselves into massive debt and danger? Are they undone by the high level of risk that comes with new ventures (even where risk is part of the attraction)? Is there something about the entrepreneurial business model that puts unholy pressure on founders of companies? Is there something peculiar in the entrepreneurial mind that predisposes founders to mental health problems? Is it that people with mental health problems are enchanted by and drawn to the entrepreneurial world with its disproportionate risk and excessive reward?

The answer to all of those questions is "perhaps," although data are emerging that help put these questions into perspective. A 2015 study by psychiatrist and entrepreneur researcher Dr. Michael Freeman, based at the University of California's San Francisco School of Medicine, found that 72 percent of entrepreneurs reported mental health concerns, and 49 percent reported having "one or more lifetime mental health conditions." This contrasts with 32 percent in the study's non-entrepreneurial comparison group. Thirty-two percent of entrepreneurs reported having two or more lifetime mental health conditions, and 18 percent reported having three or more lifetime mental health conditions. Thirty percent of entrepreneurs reported a lifetime history of depression (double the comparison group), 29 percent suffered from attention-deficit/hyperactivity disorder (ADHD) (six times the comparison group), 11 percent said they had been diagnosed with bipolar disorder (ten times the comparison group), and 12 percent reported substance abuse (three times the comparison group). Entrepreneurs were twice as likely (as the comparison group) to have attempted suicide or been hospitalized for psychiatric reasons, and far more likely to have come from families in which mental health conditions were prevalent.

Freeman's conclusion is that there is "an underlying relationship between entrepreneurship and self-reported personal and family mental health conditions." It is important to note that Freeman's data are self-reported from an entrepreneurial population disinclined to admit to any infirmity of mind, but the confidentiality of the research design enabled frankness.

These data may come as a shock to people outside the entrepreneurial community accustomed to reading stories about successful, affluent, idolized company founders in the financial press. The community itself tends to present its star practitioners in effusively commendable terms. How, one might ask, could people leading such seemingly purposeful and deeply fulfilling lives be so fragile? As we will see, this hagiographic image of entrepreneurs is often at odds with reality, as many within or on the sidelines of the entrepreneurial community know all too well.

Starting and running a venture is synonymous with a high-stress life: it heralds a relentless series of ups and downs, promising breakthroughs and inescapable setbacks, a competitive trial of intensity, sleeplessness, and exhaustion that is difficult to describe to those who have not been there. The lifestyle, in part self-imposed but also externally encouraged by an investor ecosystem that profits from draining the entrepreneurial mind of all financial value by the quickest possible route, is often one of isolation, time away from family and friends, and exposure to constant temptations—gambling, alcohol, drugs, sex with strangers, fast living.

What attracts people to the life? Sometimes it is a restless, driven brain of the sort often seen in young people with attention deficit disorder—impulsive, agitated, creative, determined. Very often, men and women in my community seem to have an abundance of energy. We think laterally and we suffer from mood swings. The minds of entrepreneurs are traditionally quick and strong but great vulnerabilities may lurk inside. These minds are capable of the brilliance that makes for impressive success but, as their ventures succeed or falter, they can succumb to uncertainty, unpredictability, narcissism, egotism, self-indulgence, greed, rivalry, and even fraud. These are accelerated minds, but for whose presence the world would be poorer.

Entrepreneurs are individuals we cannot afford to lose. They are engineers of economic growth and social progress across the industrialized world as well as in low-income countries. The OECD describes entrepreneurship as "the heart of national and local economic growth." Entrepreneurs are generally people who risk safe careers and financial security on uncertain enterprises that, when successful, create new goods, services, and employment opportunities for all. We want to see their businesses live and thrive.

Without them, there would be no novelty, no increased standard of living, no access to the possibilities that create whole new industries out of nothing.

Ever since the Industrial Revolution, we have relied on entrepreneurs to solve some of our most vexing problems, and we especially need them now because our world is currently facing large, seemingly impossible-to-solve problems. We need new sources of energy; we need prevention from new pandemics and natural disasters; and we need protection from debilitating chronic disease as the global population ages. We need deterrents to wars initiated by despots. We need new sources of food, energy, better access to health care, and job opportunities in the global south.

Entrepreneurs have roles to play in each of these challenges. Those of us in the community know we are better off when we are calm and content, not frenetic and in pain. We want our fellow entrepreneurs to take pride in their achievements but, at the same time, not to fall apart at the seams and suffer delusions of grandeur and paranoia. We want them ecstatic, but not artificially so. We want them to take risks, but not impossible risks. We don't want mania because that comes with irritability and aggression and its mirror twins, anxious depression and despair. We want our community to emit energy but not frenzy. We want competition, but also generosity and mutual support. In short, we need to nurture the well-being of entrepreneurs, this generation, and those that follow.

This book is partly my story. It starts with the observation that entrepreneurs are vulnerable to mental health challenges. I have this vulnerability. I have learned a lot about it through my studies of the brain chemical, dopamine, which, in an odd way that I'll explain in due course, has been my family's business. Dopamine is central to entrepreneurial mental health. Dopamine deficiencies manifest in depression, in lethargy, and in attention deficit disorder. Dopamine overactivity induces mania, psychotic delusions, suspicious paranoia, agitation, anxiety, and addiction. Dopamine makes what entrepreneurs do possible, and it leaves them susceptible to dangers that need to be prevented and managed. I will explain the workings of this important chemical, dopamine, which can serve as both curse and cure to accelerated minds.

Like all individuals, entrepreneurs are unique beings. We all react differently to success and failure, to the ups and downs of the entrepreneurial world. There are, however, two broad classes of entrepreneurs: those who roll with the punches and take failure as a challenge, and those who take failure personally, blame themselves, and suffer deep depressions as a consequence. The first group tends to attribute success to personal skill, and group members often feel themselves to be a cut above; they like to show off their riches and accomplishments. Members of the second group are pleased with success, but always feel they can do better. They have a mission, often many missions beyond accumulating wealth, beyond amassing possessions and awards. The stress of the entrepreneurial life affects both groups. Dopamine levels rise and fall in both. But the second group, the more ethically responsible ones, seem supersensitive to dopamine fluctuations. We will meet both groups in the pages ahead, but I am especially concerned with that second group. I hope this book can help them understand themselves better and learn practices and dodges so that they thrive in the entrepreneurial community. I also hope that, as a result of this book, the community becomes a more nurturing home for entrepreneurial talent. The book is written in tribute to entrepreneurs and in service to a world that needs to keep them healthy.

2

WHAT IS DOPAMINE?

MY PARENTS MET ON their first day of medical school at McGill University in Montreal. They met because, by coincidence, they happened to sit beside each other at the opening ceremonies. My mother was not particularly interested in my father that first day, but he was taken with her. He asked her to be in his cadaver dissection group. She said no, she had other plans. He figured out that she must have made plans with one of the other women in the class (there were only eight in the class of one hundred in 1956). So, he asked one of the other women if he could join; she said yes and that is how my parents ended up spending a lot of time together dissecting their assigned cadaver. A relative by marriage, the novelist Meyer Levin about whom I will talk later when I discuss dopamine-fuelled delusions, conceived the idea that the cadaver they dissected together over the course of the year must have been, in life, a matchmaker, a *shadchan* in Yiddish.

That anecdote is part of my own origin story, and it also offers a glimpse into what makes for success in entrepreneurship, often born of intense motivation to accomplish an important mission. My father was determined to achieve his goal and not deterred by initial failure. He found a circuitous route to get where he wanted, and relied on his intuition. He intuitively knew when he saw my mother that she was his *beshert*, his "meant to be."

Before medical school, my father had completed an under-graduate degree in physics and physiology, and then a master's degree studying the role of the salivary duct system in the forma-tion of saliva. Saliva, like dopamine, is secreted, and flows down well-mapped paths to reach its destination. Its concentration is important to health, its rate of flow matters, and the constituents of the duct through which it flows matter. There were transferable insights from the flow of saliva to understanding dopamine flow, which was destined to preoccupy him later. The head of the saliva laboratory was Professor Arnold Burgen, the youngest full professor ever at McGill University and, in the eyes of everyone who knew him, a scientific genius (later in his life, when he returned to his native England, he was knighted by the late Queen Elizabeth II). In Burgen's lab, my father learned the importance of meticulous measurement and what scientists call the dose-response curve— the critical fact that the dose of anything, be it a drug or the effort one puts into a task, matters. It's not so much *what* you do but *how much* of it you do. Too much of something good can end up, paradoxically, bad.

It was after his master's degree that my father went to McGill Medical School where he met my mother. He thought that he might be good at doctoring and curing people of disease. He was naïve. He did not realize then that doing research and healing ill people require different sorts of expertise, and a different temperament, too.

My mother also went to medical school under a misapprehension. She wanted to be a writer and thought that doctors, because patients confided in them, were in a good position to conceive of great plots for novels. It had worked for many writers she admired—Rabelais, Chekhov, Schnitzler, Somerset Maugham, Conan Doyle, Keats— so why not her? She soon realized that she was better at listening to stories others told than she was at telling them. Which is why, instead of becoming a playwright or a novelist, my mother became a psychiatrist. Had my mother and father not both mistakenly enrolled in medical school, they would never have met. Destiny works in circuitous ways.

It wasn't until the upper years of medical school at McGill, once students moved from the classroom to the hospital wards, that my father found his element. He designed several improvements in how routine lab tests were done and convinced the administration of the Montreal General Hospital to modernize its protocols; my father was a pharmacological version of a Richard Feynman–style physicist tinkerer. He was never interested in puzzles whose solution was already known. He was always looking for puzzles that no one knew the answer to. This was true during his internship, which my parents, newly married, did together in Detroit at Harper Hospital. My father kept designing better ways of doing routine procedures such as inserting needles, tubes, and catheters into various orifices. This was fortunate for my mother, who was all thumbs. She often called him over the hospital loudspeaker system for help with intern tasks that she found impossible to do on her own. It was for this reason that she chose psychiatry—no mechanical feats necessary. That, and the fascinating stories psychiatric patients told.

Before half the internship year was over, my mother knew she wanted a residency in psychiatry. My father, too, knew what he wanted. After a year of attempting to care for patients suffering from gunshot wounds, knife attacks, and addictions, he had come to recognize that practising medicine was a matter of empathy and art, while he was most interested in discovery. He knew he wanted to pursue a PhD in medical science in the hope of discovering something important.

My father spent all his free internship time searching through scientific journals for names of potential PhD supervisors and, in time, felt sure that what he wanted was a doctorate at the Rockefeller Institute in New York City under the supervision of George Palade. It is easy to see why. In one of the many obituaries written in tribute to George Palade when he died in 2008 at age 95, there is a quote from him describing the scientific atmosphere of Rockefeller around the time my father arrived: ". . . it is difficult to recapture in words the atmosphere of intense activity, remarkable achievements, great excitement, and unlimited optimism that prevailed in the laboratory, which otherwise looked like an unattractive dungeon sunk in the third basement of one of the old buildings of The Rockefeller Institute." It was in this dungeon that the modern field of cell biology was born. Palade wrote: "The new field had virtually no tradition; everybody working in it came from some other province in natural sciences . . . (there) was a pervading free spirit—often irreverent." My father fit in perfectly.

Palade had developed a technique called "cell fractionation" that could break apart cells and separate out their constituent parts according to density. He had also perfected the use of the electron microscope, which had only been invented in the 1950s. It allowed the visualization of cell constituents. The Palade lab was considered the most diversified and advanced in all the United States for biological research in electron microscopy. Afterwards, in 1974, George Palade (by that time at Yale University), together with the Belgian scientists Albert Claude and Christian de Duve, would share the Nobel Prize in Physiology and Medicine, all three men commemorated as "largely responsible for the creation of modern cell biology."

Back in 1961, my father was attracted to Dr. Palade not only as a scientist but as a person. They shared similar optimism in the promise of new discoveries, elegantly expressed by Palade in his Nobel Prize acceptance speech: "Cell biology finally makes possible a century-old dream: that of analysis of diseases at the cellular level, the first step toward their final control."

Once installed in the Palade lab, my father had to decide what to pursue for his PhD. It was an especially hot and humid summer in New York City and my mother was pregnant with my eldest brother, Marc, who was due in October 1961. She was working as a first-year resident in psychiatry at Manhattan State Hospital on Ward's Island on a schizophrenia research ward for women. My father was preoccupied and frustrated by the fact that none of the initial thesis topics suggested by Palade particularly interested him.

The preliminary experiments he attempted to conduct using the electron microscope all failed.

My mother came to his rescue. I've often thought about this—each on their own, my parents would be considered unremarkable people; together they were formidable. They leaned on each other for ideas, inspiration, support, and comfort, and the product of their shared weaknesses was strength.

My mother had not paid much attention to my father's initial PhD concerns. She was preoccupied with her pregnancy and her patients. She continued working until almost the day my brother was born. She then took a few months off, returning to her residency in January 1962. When she came back after that short absence, what forcibly struck her were the changes in the patients she had left in October. In the three months she had been away, some of her very ill patients, many of them mute and so agitated that they needed to be restrained, appeared, miraculously, much recovered. They spoke, they smiled, they welcomed her back to the ward.

The resident who had preceded my mother on the same ward was Elizabeth Kübler-Ross, who later became known for her work on death and dying. Kübler-Ross wrote about her experiences on my mother's ward at Manhattan State Hospital. She described many of the patients she met there, some my mother inherited. Psychiatric patients stayed in hospital for long periods of time in those days. Kübler-Ross wrote about one young woman who, in her late twenties, had lived on the ward for twelve years and had hardly ever spoken. She described the patient walking along the wall of the ward, head down, never looking anyone in the eye, never answering questions. This young woman later came to be in my mother's care.

Before going on pregnancy leave, my mother had prescribed a new medication. When she returned in January, she found the patient alert, still exceedingly shy and retiring but, most remarkably, no longer mute.

The new drug my mother had prescribed for her patient was one of a group of pharmaceutical agents first marketed in the early 1950s and called, at the time, "major tranquilizers." As my father paced up and down their one-bedroom apartment a few blocks north of the Rockefeller Institute in Manhattan, obsessing about what project he could do for his PhD, my mother suggested: "Why not figure out how these major tranquilizers work?"

This was the "aha!" moment for my father. The quest was challenging, it was meaningful, it was something he could do.

He could use the world's leading electron microscopy lab to study the effects of major tranquilizers on neurons (human brain cells). Neurons are thought to be the most important units of the human nervous system, which is the body's command-and-control apparatus. Neurons enable us to register information from the outside world and undertake actions in response to it. The new microscope had shown, at this point in its history, that there were gaps between brain cells, called synapses, and that the gaps were not empty: different types of neurons secreted different chemicals into these spaces and those chemicals activated adjoining neurons. These communicating chemicals were soon identified and named: acetylcholine (which is crucial to muscle control), glutamate (essential for learning and memory), gamma aminobutyric acid or GABA (which helps the brain calm down), and serotonin (which helps regulate mood and digestion, among other things). Dopamine was another.[2] These chemicals are now known as neurotransmitters and it is through them that messages are sent from one part of the brain to another and from the brain to the various parts of our bodies and from our bodies back to the brain.

My father couldn't very well extract human neurons to do his experiments so he used cells readily available—his own red blood cells. Each morning, after changing and feeding the baby, making breakfast, and preparing for work, my mother would open a new needle and syringe set. My father would roll up the sleeve of his arm and she would extract a small blood sample and transfer it to a test tube. For my parents, this peculiar almost daily ritual seemed perfectly normal. My father brought the test tube to the lab and mixed his blood with a variety of different drugs, each at a variety of doses. He then made slides of all the combinations, ran with them to the electron microscope room and plodded away at determining the effects of different drug potencies on red blood cells. Each slide was compared with a contrasting slide of my father's blood to which no drug had been added.

Red blood cells have no nucleus so there was little to see under the microscope other than round disks with membranes encircling them, each membrane composed of three layers, an outer layer and two further layers made of lipids, with protein material inside. My

2 Katherine Montagu, working in Hans Weil-Malherbe's laboratory at Runwell Hospital outside London in 1957, discovered the existence of dopamine in the brain. It belongs to a group of chemicals called catecholamines; this group also includes adrenaline and noradrenaline.

father measured the width of the membranes, and made an early discovery. When major tranquilizers were added to the blood, the membrane layer of the red blood cell expanded in width.

My father tried other drugs and found that major tranquilizers were not the only ones that expanded red cell membranes. Anaesthetics did this, too, and the membrane expansion theory of anaesthetic action was to ultimately constitute part of his PhD thesis. His interest, though, was in the psychiatric drugs. He reasoned that, by expanding the membrane of neurons as they did the membrane of red cells, these drugs decreased membrane permeability and, thus, prevented brain chemicals from entering the cell. He thought this could be how neurons were "tranquilized" and how symptoms of psychosis were alleviated. He published his membrane expansion theory in 1963 in the journal *Biochemical Pharmacology* with a young undergraduate summer student named Harvey Bialy.

In scientific discovery, as in entrepreneurship, whom you surround yourself with is critical to your success. In re-reading this study, my father's first paper in which he was lead author, I wondered what had become of Harvey Bialy. My father lost track of him after that summer studentship. At the time of the 1963 publication, Bialy was an eighteen-year-old undergraduate at Bard College. After Bard, he completed his PhD at the University of California at Berkeley and thereafter became an editor of the prestigious journal *Nature Biotechnology*. Bialy also became the author of several books of poetry, winning an arts fellowship from the US National Endowment for the Arts; and, for the rest of his life, was a controversial figure. He became one of the leading HIV denialists in the world, a small and discredited group of scientists who insisted that HIV could not be the cause of AIDS. He was a member of the widely castigated South African Presidential AIDS Advisory Panel convened by Thabo Mbeki in 2000. My father, I learned, always surrounded himself with contrarians, who were not always correct about their claims and heterodox suppositions; most were radical interdisciplinarians, which is both an advantage and a disadvantage in entrepreneurial endeavours.

My father was flush with excitement about his initial discoveries with respect to major tranquilizers. He knew there were a lot of unknowns. His plan was to pinpoint how this class of drugs worked and then figure out how they could be made both better and safer and then, knowing their mode of action, work backwards and determine the pathophysiology of psychosis and how to prevent it. This was his career plan. It was an ambitious plan given how very little scientists knew, or know now, about the intricacies of the brain.

After New York, my father completed a post-doctoral year at Cambridge University with Arnold Burgen (not yet Sir Arnold), and then opened his own lab in Toronto, devoted exclusively to the study of dopamine. He suspected that dopamine was the substance that was being blocked by the expansion (by major tranquilizers) of neuronal membranes.

Today we know a lot more about dopamine. Dopamine molecules are made and secreted from dopamine neurons; they are transported across the gap between neurons to reach neighbouring cells. Around the time my father was doing his PhD, it had been discovered that the protein layer of cell membranes was the region that housed protein receptors that "received" neurochemical molecules. To allow the reception, neurochemical transmitter molecules had to fit snugly into these receptors, which were shaped to allow entry only to specific, analogously shaped molecules. Dopamine has five differently shaped receptors that "receive" it. They are christened D1, D2, D3, D4, and D5, in sequence, according to when they were first identified and cloned.

My father then realized that it was not an expanded membrane that was doing the blocking—there was a receptor in the membrane that the drugs (now no longer called major tranquilizers but, instead, neuroleptics) were blocking. What wasn't clear was which receptor was responsible and how to find that out.

Through a long and complicated process of trial and error, my father and his lab group in the Medical Sciences building at the University of Toronto identified a receptor, in the membrane of postsynaptic cells in the part of the brain called the striatum, that fulfilled all the criteria for being the one responsible for the crucial dopamine block. This became known as the dopamine type 2 receptor (or D2). The five dopamine receptors, we now know, play important roles not only in psychosis, but also in motor movement, motivation, risk taking, addiction, cognition, and emotion. The five receptors have different tasks. The D2 and D3 receptors are the ones associated with major mental illness while the dopamine D4 receptor is associated with risk-taking and related personality traits.

What my father discovered was that the avidity with which different neuroleptics blocked the D2 receptor corresponded almost perfectly to the average clinical doses of the drugs that were effective in alleviating psychosis. "A perfect correlation? This is statistically improbable," fellow scientists told him. Nevertheless, my father and his colleagues published this remarkable correlation in the prestigious *Proceedings of the National Academy of Sciences* in 1975 and that beautiful graph has been replicated in innumerable psychiatric and psychology textbooks. It has been dubbed the most famous graph ever published in the field of psychopharmacology.

My personality has been shaped by all the men and women who preceded me, but most of all, I have been shaped by my father—by him as a person and by him as a dopamine scientist. Although he worked in neuropsychiatry—the branch of medicine that studies the relationship between mental illnesses and brain mechanisms—and was far from a businessman in the classic sense of that word, he had many entrepreneurial traits: a sense of mission, work ethic, persistence, inventiveness, and a need for like-minded colleagues, both supporters and competitors. His work has had lasting impact. He knew success—the discovery that the dopamine D2 receptor in the brain is the target for what are now known no longer as neuroleptics but as antipsychotic drugs. He knew failure, too; he did not accomplish his ultimate scientific goal, finding a cure for psychosis, and that was a deep, lasting regret for him. Such are the ups and downs of entrepreneurship. With good fortune, one day a cure will be found, and he will have made his contribution to finding it.

Neither my brothers nor I followed in our parents' footsteps: none of us went into medicine or scientific research. We tried to strike out on our own and were each, in our own ways, entrepreneurs. After my father died in 2021, I re-read many of his scientific papers and reviewed his laboratory notes for the first time. This bolstered my long-standing feeling that his work (and my mother's closely related work) had more than a passing bearing on my own life. Specifically, I was wondering whether there were links between his favourite molecule, dopamine, often referred to as the "pleasure chemical," and the various personality types I had observed in my life spent among entrepreneurs. It has been a fascinating line of inquiry.

3

HOW DOPAMINE WORKS

I BELIEVE THAT I am extra-sensitive to dopamine, and that I likely inherited this sensitivity at least in part from my mother's maternal grandfather, Abram Brzezinski. He was diagnosed with what was then called manic depression (now referred to as bipolar disorder)—which produced intense swings in energy levels and mood, and which also may have saved his family's life. It is thanks to his manic energy that he was able to engineer an escape route out of Poland for his family in January 1940, in the wake of the Nazi invasion and the persecution of the Jews. My mother would not otherwise have lived and I would not be here.

Getting out of Poland was, of course, no guarantee of safety during World War II. Safety meant getting out of Europe altogether and this was a challenge met by my maternal grandfather, Alexander Szwarc. A veteran of World War I, in 1939 he had been mobilized to fight in the Polish Army against the Germans on the western front and the Soviets on the eastern front. He was impulsive, took risks, and was tireless: when his unit was captured by the Soviets, he bribed his way out of captivity with a gold watch and made his way, somehow, to Stockholm and then to Paris. From there he persuaded the French authorities to grant French visas to his family in Poland, which is how Abram Brzezinski had been able to engineer the exit. The family thought it was safe in France but soon they had to flee again, this time to Portugal. This was made possible by the renegade Portuguese Consul, Aristedes de Sousa Mendez, who disobeyed the dictates of Portugal's dictator and worked night and day for a month, signing Portuguese transit visas for the throngs of Jews seeking escape from France.

It was, I now understand, dopamine—the chemical in the brain that encodes our experiences of pleasure and pain, risk and reward—that shaped the decisions and actions of my grandfather and great grandfather.

My mother's paternal grandfather, Issucher Szwarc, had to make lightning-fast decisions, too. He died in Zgierz, Poland, on Christmas day 1939 when German soldiers stormed his house and ransacked his library. Issucher not only collected books, he was also a prolific writer for Hebrew language newspapers and magazines. He could have yielded. He was frail and old. But, instead, he resisted.

All of us are, to some extent or another, influenced by the chemicals in our brain, especially dopamine. Understanding why and how can help us make sense of what it means to be fulfilled; to yield to temptation; to be repulsed; and to be loved.

* * *

My mother and father had three sons, of whom I'm the youngest. Because our parents had similar professional interests, dopamine played a big role in our family and among our web of friends and connections, so much so that "do-pa-mean" was the second word I spoke as a baby, the first being "book." I didn't know what dopamine meant, of course, but it was evidently something my parents had fun talking about together; it seemed to animate them. My mother would raise her voice when the topic of dopamine came up; my father would draw diagrams and wave his arms. All that told me that it was important.

I also got the impression that dopamine was something scary because I kept hearing words like "Parkinson's" and "schizophrenia" and "tremor" pop up in the midst of their conversations. I had no idea what those words meant, either, but, by the tone of my parents' voices, I could tell that trouble was attached to them. I heard "hospital," too, and that word, I knew, was bad. My parents worked in hospitals and I knew that was where sick people went.

I realized early on that dopamine represented many contrary things: it was something worth getting excited about, and it was also scary, in the same way as pain and sickness were scary. I knew from one of my childhood bedtime stories, *Pickles the Cat*, that cats could behave badly, and they could behave well, and that good and bad could be intertwined.

As time went by, I learned more about dopamine: that it plays a role in the brain not only with respect to pleasure and pain, risk and reward, and the choices people make, but that it also influences our energy, our will, and our purpose. My parents invoked dopamine to explain many of my childhood ailments, ranging from constant headaches (this was due partially, I later discovered, to my braces being too tight) and temper tantrums (I never figured out how dopamine was supposed to be implicated in those). When I got older, the temper tantrums metamorphosed into panic attacks. Still dopamine, according to my parents. "How could dopamine be so versatile?" I wondered.

Later, after law school and after graduate studies in public health, I became a restless, sleepless, serial entrepreneur, dodging bullets in a number of areas, most of them related to my emotional vulnerability and to my sense of being the target of injustice—all of which, my parents would tell me, was related to fluxes of dopamine. I think they were largely right.

I have since met and engaged with many other entrepreneurs across diverse fields, around the globe. Interesting people, often troubled. By the time I was starting to meet them and was getting to know them better, I knew a lot about dopamine. I realized that the troubles that beset so many entrepreneurs had often to do with difficulty adapting to the highs and lows of dopamine.

Dopamine is produced naturally in the brain all of the time, and sometimes released in surges. It can surge from dopamine neurons at times of stress, at times of excitement, at times of discomfort or novelty. It can surge unpredictably. Whenever there is a surge, whatever is seen, heard, smelled, touched, or tasted at the time of the surge automatically takes on special importance. It is coated with *salience*. The event that accompanies a surge, even if happenstance, remains in our memory as something meaningful. It is what we remember when other memories fade.

By attaching positive or negative importance to whatever we experience, dopamine causes us to seek out some stimuli (so as to re-experience the pleasure they originally gave us) and avoid others (if they are reminders of pain, grief, or distress). When you eat something that tastes great, the reason it tastes great is that it has stimulated a rush of dopamine in the brain. Or it may have, by happenstance, accompanied a surge. Dopamine cements memories of the experience, so one always associates that particular food with pleasure, and, thus, preferentially seeks it out.[3]

My brother, Marc, was nine years older than me and he was my role model. Still in high school, he had a glamourous job. He worked at an ice cream store, Baskin Robbins, dishing out marvelous treats to customers. He was a master of the Matterhorn, a veritable ice cream mountain that consisted of six scoops of ice cream smothered in six different sundae sauces, topped with sprinkles and nuts and whatever else he could think to put on it. That singular taste, lodged in my dopamine-induced memory, is what I equate with happiness—pure, pain-free, distress-free happiness.

Why would so much dopamine have been released when I first tasted a Matterhorn? My brothers don't share quite this same

---

3 In 2015, University of Michigan researchers Arif Hamid and Joshua Berke explained how dopamine brain levels are able to signal the value of an experience. They found that a meaning-associated memory can last a lifetime. Its effect can determine how vigorously we are motivated to work to attain a valued experience, over and over again. This can be called persistence, or it can be called addiction.

attachment to mountains of ice cream. Because they happened to get their dopamine rushes on different occasions as kids, they reminisce about other taste sensations. Perhaps, for me, it was the novelty of the Matterhorn, or the association with my big brother whom I admired so much, or simply because it tasted so damn good. The physiological reasons why some experiences in life become important to us are often mysterious. The strength of the salience that dopamine confers on chance events can be random, and the dopamine bursts, too, can come randomly. But whatever is deemed salient will matter because dopamine has decided it matters. Dopamine, in this sense, is what gives meaning to our lives—unique, personal meaning. It is how our brain encodes what matters most.

A rush of dopamine can accompany an encounter with another person, who then becomes a much sought-after source of pleasure, someone to be pursued (whether for romance, friendship, artistic collaboration, or business partnership). The pitch of someone's voice, a crooked smile—even the smell of a particular soap on their skin—can induce a dopamine avalanche fuelled by stored recollections. This effect can be all-encompassing: when certain experiences make a strong impression, other sensory impressions we have at the same time get caught up in the overall reaction. These associations act like aphrodisiacs long after the original stimulus has passed, determining whom we fall for, who inspires us, and whom we want to do business with.

This dopamine responsiveness isn't necessarily limited to direct associations: if you learn early in life that money (what my grandfather's generation called "sleet") can buy sweet-tasting food, or that sleet can buy toys, or sleet can bring adulation and respect, then making sleet induces a dopamine rush. As an adult, "making the sleet" may be what you pursue—money can become its own end, generating its own rush of pleasure, separate from the sweets or the toys you can buy with it. Because of certain formative experiences, dopamine has coated moneymaking with salience for many of us, but that alone does not decide whether or not we decide to become an entrepreneur, especially given that, as I shall discuss later, entrepreneurialism in business is not a rational path to riches.

Inspiration, motivation, incentive, stimulation, interest, inclination, desire, passion, impulse, and drive are all associated with dopamine. Dopamine shapes our choices, spurring us to act, even when the action is risky, or the investment is speculative, or the desire well beyond our reach. If our positive associations—when the pleasure of a certain experience that's been coded into our memory outweigh the hazards of pursuing it—we'll go for it. The spur can be so strong that it wins over our rational selves. It can be so strong that it propels us into danger: as we'll see, dopamine's risk-reward cycle plays an important role in many mental illnesses and addictions—and in the sometimes irreversible urge to harm oneself. Dopamine's role in impulsivity undoubtedly played a part in the suicides I referred to in the opening chapter.

My father, who knew that there were dopamine cells everywhere in the body and not only in the brain, would say that he could tell by looking at someone's eyes whether their dopamine levels were high at the time—whether the individuals were able to drum up the energy to stay up all night and work if they were asked to (he needed to know that about his students). The fast eye blink rate would give them away because that's yet another bodily function governed by dopamine.

High levels of dopamine result in high energy, strong reactions to our environments, and lots of blinking. Low levels of dopamine result in slow responses and blunted interest. It follows that dopamine and mental health are deeply connected. Too little dopamine in the brain can cause mental health problems such as indifference, lethargy, and Parkinson's disease; too much dopamine can cause high anxiety, addiction, and hallucinations. Good mental health among entrepreneurs depends on achieving dopamine balance. Later I will discuss the tools that can make that possible.

Dopamine balance is harder to achieve for some than for others; self-critical entrepreneurs who yearn for ever-greater accomplishments tend to be people who find balance elusive. Because everyone is different, our responsiveness to the transmission of dopamine varies substantially. Some of us quickly adapt to changing levels of dopamine in our brains, while others are sensitive to the flux, and overreact.

Dopamine can be knocked off balance, it can be suppressed, accelerated, or high-jacked. An imbalance or dysregulation can result from inborn gene variations, prenatal and early childhood experiences, disabilities, infections, traumas, bereavements, or natural disasters. When dopamine is heavily dysregulated, we tend to lose our usual rational grip on things, and ability to make wise decisions. Our perception of risk and reward gets distorted. What normally gives us pleasure brings, instead, grief. We may suffer delusions and paranoia. As we'll see, there are many unfortunate health outcomes of dopamine dysregulation, and they show up with alarming frequency in the entrepreneurial community.

4

THE DANGERS OF DOPAMINE

ONE REASON THAT DOPAMINE is particularly powerful is that it acts on a key brain structure called the hippocampus, which is responsible for memory storage. This allows dopamine to determine what we remember and what we forget. (Anatomists of the past thought the hippocampus looked like a sea horse, which explains its name, from the Greek: *hippos* for horse, and *kampos* for sea monster.) For better or worse, our fundamental beliefs are based on what we remember and store as memories in the hippocampus—on whatever dopamine coats with enough salience, often at a very early age, and makes permanent.

I will always, for example, remember the technologically significant number, 82767. We had an Apple 1 computer at home when I was a kid and that is the highest number to which it could count. Bob, the middle brother, worked in a computer store, so we had been able to purchase the computer well before it was widely available to consumers. This, of course, was very exciting to ten-year-old me. Bob made a joystick using a broken car stick shift, so my two brothers and I could play Space Invaders—the 1.0 version with tiny white exclamation marks and asterisks to illustrate invading aliens. The reason I can tell you all this in such detail more than forty years later? Dopamine.

Dopamine is also why I remember that one day in March 1981, while I was playing Space Invaders on that Apple 1 computer with my friend Mark, a man named John Hinckley Jr. tried to assassinate US president Ronald Reagan. It registered as an important moment, and the memory got encoded for life.

"Why did Hinckley want to kill Reagan?" I asked my Mom later. My mother, the psychiatrist, said he suffered from de Clérambeault's syndrome, a form of delusional thinking that made you believe that someone totally out of your league romantically, someone glamourous and famous, was in love with you. Victims of this syndrome believed they could tell they were loved by someone—specifically, someone famous—just from the way the famous person's eyes seemed to focus on them from the movie screen or magazine photo. In Hinckley's case, the famous person, in his mind in love with him, was the actor, Jodie Foster. He must have thought that if he came to national attention by doing something like assassinating the President (this was loosely modelled on the plot of a movie Foster had been in) he would become her equal.

Dopamine was partially responsible for this crime. Dopamine makes you think big; you feel compelled by some larger force to act on your impulse. Often, though not in this case, dopamine makes you think big in a good way—in an ambitious, positive way. Dopamine can fuel you. The trouble, as so many people learn, is at the extremes—if you have far too little dopamine coursing through your body, or too much. And, again, some of us are more sensitive than others to both the chemical's flow rate, and to its fluxes.

* * *

I've mentioned that many of my mother's patients—the ones who were helped so profoundly by dopamine-dampening antipsychotic drugs—had a psychotic diagnosis. People with these disorders are reported to have an excess of dopamine in some parts of the brain. They experience a variety of symptoms, the best known and most distressing of which are delusions and hallucinations. Delusions and hallucinations can also be triggered by alcohol and drugs of abuse. I have learned that, to understand entrepreneurial ambitions, it is crucial to understand delusions. For it is surely a form of delusion to believe yourself, as an entrepreneur, inexorably capable of manipulating events in a way that will "dent the universe" as Steve Jobs envisioned.

The other feature of psychosis is hallucination. A hallucination is not a belief, but a sense perception. It is an experience of seeing or hearing or smelling or tasting or feeling with no objective cause. In the context of a disorder such as schizophrenia, hallucinations are most often auditory and patients refer to them as "voices." The hallucination can take the form of a comment or an insult, or a criticism, or a series of audible obscenities. At times, though, voices can be supportive and encouraging, flattering, morale boosting.

The most dangerous voices are those that give commands that, patients report, can feel so compelling that they have no choice but to obey. Such commands may instruct the patient to commit acts of violence and may precipitate suicide attempts.

A delusion, on the other hand, is an idiosyncratic belief that defies external reality but is clung to despite evidence that it is false.[4] The word "idiosyncratic" (from the Greek word, *idiosynkrasia*, meaning "a peculiar temperament") is considered critical in distinguishing what is now called "neurotypic" behaviour from pathological behaviour. The word "normal" is no longer used because there is nothing abnormal about these phenomena—they are as prevalent as the common cold. People who consider themselves free from all mental quirks are non-neurotypic or insufficiently self-aware or, simply, yet to be diagnosed. As the saying goes, the only people who are normal are the ones we don't know very well.

---

4 The philosopher Ian Gold of McGill University and his psychiatrist brother, Joel Gold, of New York University delineate twelve categories of delusion in *Suspicious Minds: How Culture Shapes Madness*: "(1) persecutorial delusions, which are concerned with being harmed by others; (2) referential delusions—beliefs that events in the environment are directed at the delusional individual or have a special meaning for him; (3) grandiose delusions, according to which one is exceptional or powerful; (4) erotomanic delusions—beliefs that someone is in love with the delusional person; (5) nihilistic delusions, which are concerned with an imminent catastrophe or with nonexistence of some kind . . .; (6) somatic delusions—concerns about one's health and bodily function; (7) delusions concerning thoughts being withdrawn from, or inserted into, one's mind; (8) delusions of control, according to which one's body or actions are being manipulated by another agent; (9) delusions of jealousy (also known as Othello syndrome), beliefs that one's partner is unfaithful; (10) religious delusions, according to which one is either being persecuted by supernatural forces or is on a divine mission; (11) delusions of guilt or sin—beliefs that one is responsible for some disaster or tragedy; and (12) misidentification delusions, which are concerned with the identity of other people."

Delusional beliefs commonly associated with mental illness or substance abuse revolve around being followed, or feeling that others are reading your thoughts, or sensing the presence of ghosts at night, or wrongly interpreting supposed proof of spousal infidelities, or experiencing bodily distortions. Not all false beliefs are judged to be delusions. The claim that the measles, mumps, and rubella vaccines cause autism or, more recently, that wearing masks against COVID-19 is bad for your health, are too widely held to be considered delusions. Similarly, extreme entrepreneurial convictions, for instance, that money can be made quickly, even without a sellable product, cannot be called delusions either, because they run rampant in today's entrepreneurial world. Nowadays, money *is* actually being made on no tangible basis if you consider the many zero-revenue unicorns that sell shares in the private markets at an implied company valuation of more than one billion dollars, something I will expand upon later.

Some hallucinations seem similar to relatively common experiences, such as hearing the voice of a loved one after they've died. And some delusions are somewhat believable: for example, that your boss takes pleasure in humiliating you in front of others. Others—that the dentist has planted radio transmitters into your fillings—are not. What is crucial to note is that all these false beliefs and perceptions are important to the person who believes them. No matter the content of the hallucination or delusion, it is persistent; it remains lodged for long periods of time at the back of a person's mind.

Put another way, when someone suffers from delusions or hallucinations, a dysregulation of dopamine has coated their false sensations and beliefs with overwhelming salience. It isn't just that dopamine has become associated with odd experiences, it's that it has imbued them with absolute, unique importance.

* * *

How are delusions and hallucinations treated? They can be remedied by the same kind of drugs as those that seemed to work so miraculously on my mother's ward in New York City back in 1961. Though my mother had been extremely impressed by the effectiveness of the drugs, and, because of that, had convinced my father to study them, she nevertheless knew that their effects were not all positive. The young woman who had gone, after twelve years in hospital, from being totally withdrawn and silent to engaging in conversation? She unfortunately developed a tremor and a stiff gait, as well as a form of muscle rigidity, side effects reminiscent of Parkinson's disease.

Parkinsonian side effects induced extreme agitation in many of my mother's patients: they couldn't stop moving. They experienced a form of agitation (called akathisia) that many found intolerable. One patient, after receiving an injection of a medication that was formulated to last for two weeks in the body, spent that entire period, seemingly night and day, pacing up and down the hospital corridor in distress. Another was so tormented by akathisia that, on a weekend pass from hospital, she jumped off her balcony to her death. One seventeen-year-old patient had an opisthotonic crisis, a severe muscular spasm of her neck during which her head forcibly arched backward and cut off her airway, causing her death. These were catastrophic events.

My mother learned that drugs that do wonders can also kill. These were still early days in the treatment of psychotic illness. There were no guidelines or protocols that instructed doctors on what doses to use. The head of my Mom's ward believed in very high doses, as did many clinicians in the field at that time. Dose, as my father well knew from his scientific training, is all-important in drug prescribing. Doctors know now that starting doses of antipsychotic drugs to treat dopamine dysregulation have to be low and increments have to be gradual. This goes for many things in life, not just therapeutic drugs. My mother, when on that ward, often secretly advised patients to take only half their prescribed dose.

In Toronto, when I was growing up, I came to know some of my mother's patients. I noticed that many were overweight, but the side effect that stood out for me was the jerkiness of their hands, the tremors, the mouth movements, a neurological condition that my father said was called tardive dyskinesia. "Why are your patients so spastic?" I recall asking my Mom. This was another side effect that, by blocking the transmission of dopamine, mimicked the signs of Parkinson's disease. This was not coincidental: Parkinson's is a disease of dopamine deficiency.

The person who, in 1960, discovered that Parkinson's disease was a disease of dopamine deficiency was a young Viennese researcher named Oleh Hornykiewicz. Professor Hornykiewicz made this discovery by examining patients' post-mortem brains and comparing them with the brains of patients who had died of neurological diseases other than Parkinson's. He then gave L-Dopa (or levodopa), a dopamine precursor amino acid that is able to enter the brain, to living Parkinson's patients. What he found was that their muscle stiffness, spasms, and finger tremors dramatically improved.[5]

Today, it is generally agreed that Dr. Hornykiewicz's idea of treating Parkinson's disease with L-Dopa represents one of the greatest triumphs of pharmacology in history and marks the start of the era of neurotransmitter-based therapeutics. After his great discovery in Vienna, Hornykiewicz spent ten years, from 1967 to 1977, at the University of Toronto, working in the same department of pharmacology as my father. From this ensued a close friendship and scientific collegiality. With Dr. Hornykiewicz and my father in the same department, Toronto became the world centre of dopamine science.

In the 1970s, to be a dopamine scientist was to be a member of a small club. When I was five—another indelible memory—I noticed a cluster of scientists standing around our newly arrived Maytag dishwasher. It was one of my father's traditional Sunday afternoon gatherings to which the staff of his department were invited. My parents later explained to me that automatic dishwashers were still

---

5 L-Dopa rose to public prominence with the 1990 film *Awakenings*, which won Oscar awards for Best Picture and Best Actor in 1991. Robin Williams was superb as Dr. Oliver Sacks, the real-life neurologist who had worked at Mount Carmel outside New York City and treated eighty patients with what was then called "intractable Parkinsonian syndrome." The syndrome was described as "patients trapped inside themselves"—until L-Dopa sprung the trap. Williams suicided at age 63. He had been diagnosed with Parkinson's but was dying of Lewy body disease, a related disorder in which chemical changes in the brain interrupt the production of dopamine and cause problems with thinking, movement, behaviour, and mood.

something of a novelty then, beyond the reach of most ill-paid university professors. Dr. Hornykiewicz and his wife, Christina, had been among the first to own a dishwasher. They had four children and a lot of dishes to wash. Dr. Hornykiewicz had become expert in the art of efficiently stacking dishes in parallel racks. He was demonstrating his technique to the others. I had been told he was a great scientist, so, in my mind, this is what great scientists did—they stacked their dishes in a scientifically ordered fashion. Once, when one of my classmates asked me if my father was truly a mad scientist—for kids all over the world, any scientist worthy of the name is a mad one—I said, "I don't know. In our house my mother stacks the dishes."

Because the treatment for Parkinson's disease consists of medications that boost dopamine, patients often undergo a variety of dopamine-related side effects, the worst of which are probably hallucinations. Other effects can be deeply disruptive as well: to the consternation of family members, when people with Parkinson's disease are treated, they get impulsive and compulsive, they often start to gamble, sometimes recklessly, and commit sexual indiscretions. Older women I've known feel humiliated when their aging partners, in treatment for Parkinson's, can't stop themselves from making crude remarks to young waitresses at restaurants, or to vulnerable female students.

A family friend who was a well-respected piano instructor in Montreal developed Parkinson's disease, and was treated with a dopamine-like drug. He subsequently lost his female students, one by one, because he inappropriately fondled their fingers when teaching. The fault in these cases often lies partially with induced dopamine dysregulation—an unfortunate consequence of trying to supplement the body's dopamine deficiency. The man is under the sway of excess dopamine that makes him remember old pleasures and, in a sense, coerces him to repeat them. The responsibility, of course, is still his, but it shows what dysregulated dopamine can do to permit the expression of an unacceptable impulse.

Dopamine needs to be balanced. Again, our ability to accurately assess risks and rewards, costs and benefits, depends upon this balance, as does our experience of pleasure and pain. For most of us, if we are flooded too quickly with dopamine, or if our bodies aren't making enough of it, we suffer, and make others around us suffer as well.

There's a dopamine analogy to online shopping. If you've ever found yourself coping with a bad day by going on an unplanned online shopping spree, or if you've developed a habit of buying things online that you don't particularly need or want, out of nothing more than sheer boredom, you'll know what I mean. You visit a website you like, one you've been to before. Conveniently, it remembers your previous purchases—and every time you go back to the site, it tempts you with new ads and offers of similar items. This is an algorithm borrowed from dopamine circuitry. Nowadays, it is built into the code of many social media platforms, and most of the most popular gaming apps, too.

In this same way, dopamine facilitates the repetition of an originally gratifying action, even when the action no longer brings pleasure. Such impulses can be resisted, but not easily. In a landmark 1971 essay, American social scientists Philip Brickman and Donald Campbell coined the term "hedonic treadmill." As with the more mundane treadmills you might see in a gym, a hedonic treadmill is one that doesn't get you anywhere: you run, but you never change your location. Brickman and Campbell were writing about the unceasing pursuit of self-indulgence, with the implication that staying on that particular hedonic-style treadmill does not get you far; you end up where you began.

Similarly, short-acting drugs of abuse, such as cocaine or amphetamine, though far more destructive than a natural uptick in dopamine, stimulate the quick-shot release of dopamine; their effects include increased movement, pronounced motor agitation, and impulsivity, as well as intense pleasure. By quickly flooding your brain with dopamine, they result in delusions, hallucinations, and addiction.

* * *

There is a connection between addiction and impulsivity. Human beings vary in their capacity to predict the potential consequences of their actions and to think before they act. Some find decisions very difficult and deliberate for a long time before selecting and committing to a course of action. Others habitually make rash, sometimes destructive decisions on what appear to be whims. They are impulsive, with a tendency to act without thinking. Since dopamine is so involved in our perceptions of risk and reward, it is not surprising to learn that it is involved in impulsivity, too. Dopamine is specifically implicated in cognitive control and cognitive flexibility (the ability to appropriately adapt one's decisions to the circumstances at hand). The dopamine cells of impulsive people, especially when they are exposed to a novel or rewarding stimulus, fire at split-second rates.

What kind of stimulus counts as a reward? It can be anything— whatever you find enticing or whatever elicits a rush of good memories. The flashing ads at an online store might be one. So could the glimpse of an ice-cream sundae as you walk past a diner that tempts you to veer off course and duck inside to order one. In popular culture, there's a clichéd depiction of a man in the middle of his life, feeling set in his ways, perhaps bored or stuck, who shows up in the driveway one day in a new sports car. That's impulsivity, fuelled by dopamine.

Impulsivity, researchers have found, is often correlated with aggression—which is usually regarded as a negative trait, but has been crucial to our survival as a species. Human beings exist because our ancestors were aggressive in defending territory, killing predators, and competing with each other for food and mating opportunities. Aggressiveness is required to protect offspring and kin in skirmishes and wars; it is sometimes vital in resolving disputes. Two circuits in the brain, both involving dopamine, modulate aggression, and animal studies have demonstrated the essential role of dopamine signals in assessing when to use aggressive tactics. Verbal aggression is a requisite, at appropriate times, in a fiercely competitive field like entrepreneurship. Dopamine reinforces aggressive behaviours by making them feel pleasurable and, therefore, rewarding.

We are all both impulsive and aggressive at times, and this is especially so for entrepreneurs. Many of us have also harboured grandiose or paranoid thoughts that rise close to, if not right up to, the level of delusions. Whether distressing or aggrandizing, what all delusions have in common is that the person with the delusion plays a focal role, the protagonist role either as victim or hero. From what is known today about the salience-coating effect of dopamine makes it understandable that an increase in dopamine transmission in the brain could well convince a person that the world revolves around them (after all, many people feel that way even when not delusional). Being at the centre of something, even something bad, is ego-boosting, which is why delusions are so impervious to change. Others saying it's not true doesn't move the needle at all. Perhaps this is why it is so difficult for entrepreneurs to walk away from a failing venture. You believe, delusionally, that you can save it if you only try harder.

An interesting question is whether delusions are always, as widely believed, pathological and dangerous. My great grandfather Issucher Szwarc was undoubtedly delusional when he thought he could protect his precious collection of ancient texts in Zgierz, Poland, in December 1939 from the Nazi flames. He failed. My great grandfather, Abram Brzezinski, was certainly delusional when he thought he could smuggle his family out of German-occupied Poland. He succeeded. There are delusions that are pleasant and make a person feel important, such as believing that the mayor of your city has fallen in love with you, that your classmates are jealous of you because of your beauty or brilliance, or that you are the reincarnation of a famous historical figure, whether Jesus Christ or Cleopatra or Winston Churchill. But even unpleasant, frightening delusions can make you feel important.

My mother had a cousin named Tereska Torrès. Tereska, a writer herself, married a best-selling novelist, Meyer Levin. He was an established author and had produced and directed a famous film, *Exodus,* about postwar Jews leaving Europe for Palestine (with Tereska in the starring role). Because he was already known in the literary world for his earlier Jewish-themed books, Levin in 1952 was approached by Otto Frank, Anne Frank's father, to write a book review of the English translation of *The Diary of a Young Girl.* He wrote an extraordinary piece published on the front page of the *New York Times Review of Books.* It began: "Anne Frank's diary is too tenderly intimate a book to be frozen with the label 'classic,' and yet no lesser designation serves. For little Anne Frank, spirited, moody, witty, self-doubting, succeeded in communicating in virtually perfect, or classic, form the drama of puberty. But her book is not a classic to be left on the library shelf. It is a warm and stirring confession, to be read over and over from insight and enjoyment." Thanks to this glowing review, the *Diary* subsequently took the world by storm.

Levin later wrote a dramatic version of *The Diary,* originally destined for Broadway. When potential investors read his script, however, they judged it to be "too Jewish." Broadway wanted something more universal, about man's inhumanity to man, not simply man's inhumanity to Jews. A universally pleasing play was eventually produced and turned into a film, using a script that had been adapted from Anne Frank's diary by other writers. A number of lawsuits followed, with suits and countersuits and accusations of plagiarism. Ultimately, Levin publicly vilified everyone associated with the theatrical and film versions of the book and was vilified in turn. Levin's preoccupation with these events eventually became a full-blown entrepreneurial obsession that turned into a delusion.

The world, he thought, was against him. But he argued his point trenchantly, that Anne Frank hiding in a Dutch attic was a quintessentially Jewish story. It was an important point of view. Who's to say whether or not the propagation of this important message made his mental health struggles worthwhile?

Having delusions, becoming obsessed, suffering anxieties, demonstrating impulsivity: all these have negative connotations, and all can be damaging in their severe forms. It is also true that many people having these experiences—including entrepreneurs— can overcome them, and accomplish good things in their careers and in their lives. And so, accomplishment should not be pitted against mental health. As I shall show later in this book, entrepreneurial accomplishment and mental health can readily coexist.

Grandiose delusions loom large in the entrepreneurial community. In my experience, entrepreneurs are particularly vulnerable to feeling grander than others. They see themselves as touched by inspiration in unique ways, as if called upon to dent the universe in the way Steve Jobs imagined. Some harbour delusions about what they can do for the world—visions that are often considered heroic. These ambitious delusions, often wildly improbable, sometimes succeed. Entrepreneurs are also susceptible to paranoid delusions about a competitor encroaching on their customers or copying products or stealing intellectual property, or seeking to hire away their best employees. This form of strategic paranoia can be good for the firm's survival and longevity, but not for the mental health of the entrepreneur.

What makes dopamine so tricky to manage in the entrepreneurial world is its association with the most intensely pleasurable moments of your life, motivating you to your highest levels of performance and most fulfilling achievements. But it can leave you feeling unregulated, depressed, and addicted or, as we saw in the opening chapter, far worse than that. And it is often difficult to control dopamine-fuelled behaviour. At any given moment or circumstance, any of us can yield to wild dopaminergic impulses.

5

WHAT IS AN ENTREPRENEUR?

ARC ROBERTS IS A renowned sociologist who used to teach management theory and social psychology at Harvard. He loved teaching, and his teaching style was unique. Students said when he retired that they viewed the world differently after attending a course with Roberts. He engaged his students intellectually, ethically, and on a personal level. He taught difficult management concepts in novel ways. I was one of about 100 graduate students in his class in the spring of 1998. One day, without advance notice, he divided the class into two groups: judges and participants. As instructed, the fifty or so participants, of which I was one, divided ourselves into teams of five or six. Each team was asked to march up to small tables near the blackboard at the front of the classroom. On each table were envelopes, staplers, a staple remover, elastic bands, papers, paper clips, rolls of tape, and manicured, laser-printed address labels, along with some brief instructions.

The instructions were not really instructions. They were statements telling us what students in previous years had done in the time allotted with these very same materials. There was no indication as to what should be done, only what had, in the past, been done, and that was very diversified. It seemed we could take whatever approach we wanted to these staples, papers, and envelopes but, whatever we ended up doing, the groups were in competition with each other. Professor Roberts explained that in past years some teams were judged on speed and other teams on orderliness, still others on enthusiasm. So we had a task that was to be completed in thirty minutes. We didn't know what the task was, and we didn't know what the competition was about.

Several teams started by appointing a leader, creating a team name and even a team cheer. (I remember one Princeton grad with a loud voice egging his team on, like a cox on a rowing team coursing down the Charles River against rivals from Harvard.) Meanwhile, the judges were asked to watch quietly and take notes about the different teams' approaches to handling the assignment.

After thirty minutes we returned to our seats and Roberts told us that this "experience" had been a feature of his class for more than twenty years. He never actually told us what it was meant to teach us; I think we were meant to learn something about ourselves, our leadership styles, our group interaction skills, our responses to uncertainty. Over the years, various experts had assessed the outcomes from a variety of perspectives, he said. Scholars, we were told, had analyzed the results through a feminist lens: men, they found, tended disproportionately to handle the "tools" (these being the staplers, staple removers, elastic bands, and paperclips), in line with traditional views of masculinity, while women tended to package the paper into envelopes (a sign of nesting or organizing associated with self-reinforced traditional understandings of femininity). Strategic analysis of team packaging skill had also been done. Efforts at creating team solidarity, like team names and chants, did not, apparently, improve either speed, grace, or orderliness.

After telling us this, Roberts paused and said, "And now, I'd like to spend ten minutes talking about Neil's behaviour." He was pointing at me and smiling. "Every year we have someone like Neil," Roberts continued, "but this is a particularly extreme and interesting case. Neil pointed out to his teammates that the assignment was in fact not an assignment—that they were not being graded on it—and that the instructions were not instructions, merely indications of what past guinea pigs in the class had done. He told his group that the concept of team chants was juvenile. And he convinced them to let the envelopes sit untouched, and instead to go for coffee and get to know each other better."

"In every business organization," Roberts said, "you'll always have a rebel to manage, someone like Neil; they always leave the company after one or two years or less. The manager's goal is to eke as much value out of them as possible, if possible at all, before they leave. They tend to go off in a huff and start something new; they may succeed or they may, more likely, fail repeatedly, but they're always happiest after they leave."

So what does this say about me? That I'm a contrarian, a rule breaker, a persuasive guy, an odd ball, an intuitive person who realized that the point of the experience was to build team spirit, or simply someone who couldn't be bothered with an assignment that didn't "count," who only worked if there was a payoff? Those interpretations may all be true, but my understanding of dopamine suggests I'm just a bit different than others in what motivates me to work, to the extent that I only want to do things that are meaningful to me and be around those who share that meaning. Meaning, to my mind, is an entrepreneurial impulse; we gain reward by finding it.

* * *

In the entrepreneurial community, we all just want to be a little bit like Benjamin Franklin. Benjamin Franklin is widely regarded as America's first entrepreneur. His astonishing capacity for invention, and re-invention, was evident early on. The young Franklin had been apprenticed at age twelve to his older half-brother James, a printer; in short order he began submitting essays that were published under the pseudonym Silence Dogood. In 1723, Franklin moved to Philadelphia, where he started his own newspaper (the *Pennsylvania Gazette*), a subscription library, a philosophical society, a fire company, a hospital, and a militia. He served as postmaster of the city, established an academy that later became the University of Pennsylvania, created bifocal spectacles, the stove, and a water harmonica. In 1752, he invented the lightning rod, which led to his induction into the Royal Society in London and to several honorary degrees. He helped draft and sign the *Declaration of Independence*, gained France's support for American independence in 1778, and negotiated the treaty of peace with Britain in 1783. To top this off, his autobiography, first published in 1791 in Paris as *Mémoires*, is considered one of the finest works of writing in all of history. His is an example to admire, to emulate.

Contemporary culture tends to define entrepreneurs as people who create start-ups with enormous sums of venture capital money; media outlets often fixate on young tech entrepreneurs and start-up *wunderkinds*, lone geniuses who revolutionize entire industries on the strength of their insights. That is a fashionable modern definition. It is also inaccurate and causes many problems.

The entrepreneurs who live in the popular imagination of the small but influential financial and start-up tech media do satisfy the basic criteria of starting something new and employing people. Yet this constitutes a tiny slice of entrepreneurship. For starters, neither the field of endeavour nor the age of the creator is pertinent. Founders of enterprises tend to be in the middle of their working lives and the financial success and the longevity of their ventures is often positively correlated with relevant experience. Entrepreneurs exist in all sectors, and are interested in working across the full spectrum of human activity.

When people think of famous entrepreneurs, it's the likes of Elon Musk and Richard Branson that come easiest to mind. But the activist singer-songwriter Neil Young is every bit as much an entrepreneur. He has all the characteristics: starting as a solo act, founding and co-founding bands, dropping in and out of bands, and always following his own notions of what's interesting and valuable. In addition to his long career in music, Young has been part owner of Lionel, a company that makes model railroad trains and accessories. Though his shares in the company vaporized after it emerged from bankruptcy, Young stayed involved, sitting on its board of directors and becoming hyper-focused on the design of the Lionel Legacy control system for model trains. He is listed as a co-inventor on seven US patents related to this field. Few of these ventures could have made him a fortune, even theoretically. That's not why he's in it. He is a tireless and contrarian enthusiast of innovation; his personal website is called the *NYA* [Neil Young Archives] *Times-Contrarian*. To my mind, he's a model entrepreneur.

Boiled down to their essential components, entrepreneurs are those who generate new ideas and innovations, always convinced that the status quo can be improved. They are forever hunting for ways to do things faster or better or more efficiently. They live to solve problems that bring lasting value to their communities. They are typically restless, happy to go against the grain, not infrequently self-confident to the point of bombast, and aggressive verbally and in what they write. Their minds are usually on overdrive, racing with inspirations and ideals. They manifest higher-than-average tolerance for uncertainty and risk. They enjoy the process of enormously complicated decision-making.

A certain degree of emotional flexibility is useful to cope with the entrepreneurial journey, and congeniality is important, although many are limited in this regard by their need for independence. I've seen a lot of entrepreneurs choose work independence not necessarily because they are independent thinkers, but because they don't know how to get on with bosses, they don't know how to adapt to someone giving them orders. They choose entrepreneurship because of a deficit, not a strength. Other deficits that may lead to this career choice have been posited: a tendency to self-indulgence, a proneness to anxiety, a poor attention span, a high degree of competitiveness (sibling rivalry is often a reason), an inordinate need for adulation, or an obsessive personality that requires things to be done one way only (their way).

Entrepreneurs are not necessarily the most rational of people. In fact, becoming an entrepreneur is not a rational decision. You're trying to produce something new. Nobody knows how it will turn out because there are no exact precedents for what you're undertaking (if there were, it probably wouldn't be as interesting to you). By launching a new venture, you're committing to serious responsibility, chronic uncertainty, long hours, and lost weekends and holidays. The financial odds are against you. Your journey, statistically speaking, is unlikely to get you where you aim to go (my entrepreneur coach, Srikanth, used to remind me that entrepreneurial leadership is about "letting people down at the rate they can handle"). Most of your ambitious attempts are flops; entrepreneurship, in its essence, is about *failure*, which is why so many find it a difficult lifestyle to adopt and eventually drop out of the race. The costs of perceived failure, as we saw in the first chapter, can be calamitous.

So why are people still willing—eager, even—to sign up for entrepreneurship given the long odds of success and the better odds of loss and personal damage? Why do some entrepreneurs persist with the agony and economic burden their ventures bring even after repeated failure? Would it make more sense to join your classmates and neighbours in appreciating the relative certainty of job security and financial rewards that come with a traditional career and family life? To a rational third-party observer, entrepreneurs can appear unhinged. There are almost always easier ways to go through life and to achieve your goals than entrepreneurship. Imagine you have an idea for how to cure a particular type of cancer. Does it really make sense to found a company and try to raise $100 million for this new venture from investors who want to see a quick return on their investment? Wouldn't you be better off graduating from a top science program and settling in at a well-resourced cancer specialty hospital?

The choice to become an entrepreneur is often not rational. Steven Pinker, the Harvard cognitive psychologist, defines rationality as the utilization of accumulated knowledge to reach goals that hold personal meaning. There is important nuance in this definition that my friend Patrick Luciani, an economist, explained to me. "Rationality cannot tell you what it is you want," said Patrick. "It can only tell you how to get it. If I decide I want to rob a bank, I use my reason to figure out how to do it without getting caught. But the initial decision to rob a bank has nothing to do with rationality. It's about preferences. Once you've emotionally decided on what you want, only then do you weigh the costs and benefits of the mini-decisions you make to rob the bank effectively."

The truth is that entrepreneurs often can't help themselves refrain from taking risks. In the 1940s, Austrian-American economist Joseph Schumpeter was the first to invoke a picture of entrepreneurs as "wild spirits." He described them as "fiery souls" engaged in a process of "creative destruction" that could result in new industries and transform everyday life. By my definition or by Schumpeter's—and, again, in contrast with contemporary depictions of a lone genius running a globe-spanning technology behemoth—entrepreneurs can be understood simply as creators of for-profit or not-for-profit ventures, usually but not always in partnership with colleagues. Their aim is to accelerate innovation and exert major impact, in other words, to make the dent that Jobs evangelized as a noble cause.

No matter the risk, the entrepreneurial aim is to come up with an idea or create a product to which others—ideally, hundreds of thousands or millions of others—attach value. This is crucial: entrepreneurs cannot, and do not want, to exist in a vacuum. What distinguishes them from the broader class of tinkerers is that they want to see the impact of their work manifest in the world, and in the people they care about. When it comes to the entrepreneurial labour market, Roger Martin, the business author, academic, and former dean of the University of Toronto's Rotman School of Business, advised me in November 2013: There are three communities you care about: yourself, how you appear to the broader community, and, most important, how you appear to the small community you care about most. Martin told me this as I was angling to convince him of the cleverness of various new business ideas I had at the time. His was an important insight—one that proved to be crucial in my understanding of what makes entrepreneurs tick and what can push them too far.

What is the "small community" entrepreneurs care about most? One example is the like-minded dopamine scientists clustered around the dishwasher in my childhood home. Another is The Beatles. The entrepreneurial community they cared about, even as they were breaking up, consisted of their bandmates. Sir Paul McCartney was asked, when he appeared at the Liverpool Institute of Performing Arts in July 2018, which musicians he most admired and why. "Fellow Beatles," he answered, as if this should be obvious to anyone: "John, who was pretty cool, and George and Ringo. Having worked with John so one-on-one, I got to see his [songs] before the world did. I'm a big fan." He said this despite the infamous acrimony that later arose among the former bandmates.

Entrepreneurs are not altruists even if they do sometimes have altruistic aims. They seek personal rewards, or the promise of rewards. They are happy to make money. "When the cash flow is full," said my entrepreneurial friend and dopamine researcher Craig Hudson, "that's certainly a dopaminergic feeling. And certainly what you do needs to make business sense, be aligned toward profit, otherwise there is no impact to enable the other things that matter more." The point is that other things do matter more. Making money is not that high on the list of rewards most entrepreneurs seek. More than anything, they are people who want desperately to live up to or exceed the expectations of specific others in their community. That is why the people we most closely associate with, our communities, are so important. And entrepreneurial communities are swelling in number across all major economies.

* * *

There is growing evidence that entrepreneurship is on the rise across industrialized countries. New business applications reached a record 5.3 million in the United States in 2021, up from about 4 million in 2020. And at the end of 2021, the number was slated to grow again: Intuit Quickbooks released a study in December

2021 that estimated that 17 million people in the United States planned to start new small businesses in 2022. Nearly half of all Americans—47.5 percent—are now employed in small businesses.

David Woo, the macroeconomist and former top Wall Street trader, told me he thinks the reason entrepreneurialism has shot up in the midst of the pandemic is largely due to the fact that, in an age of labour market turmoil, people want more control of their lives. According to a 2022 small business study by Guidance Financial, 55 percent of US small-business owners cited that as their main motivator. This was followed by 39 percent who said their motivation was pursuing their passion.

What all this tells me is that despite the considerable challenges faced by start-up small businesses amid COVID-19, entrepreneurial activity remains robust; the passion to build something new is part of our evolutionary imperative, and persists despite—and sometimes even especially in—hard times.

Perhaps the biggest limiting factor to entrepreneurship—the hurdle anyone with a good idea has to clear—is financing. The reality is that all entrepreneurs need money, usually quite a lot of money, to get their businesses off the ground. Just as I remember my father spending all his free time writing grant applications to finance his dopamine research ("Three applications per experiment," he used to tell me, "because two out of three will fail"), so do entrepreneurs need to spend a great deal of their scarce time figuring out how to raise money to keep their businesses afloat.

This can make entrepreneurs seem preoccupied with money and gives rise to the misperception that profit is their sole goal. It may surprise readers to know that most entrepreneurs are not particularly well off. They generally suffer through many years of low earnings while their venture is getting off the ground; even if their company does ultimately succeed, they are saddled with debt. Should a company mature beyond that, into a much larger, wildly successful venture, their investor backers and early employees often profit much more than they themselves do. Statistically speaking, founder entrepreneurs have lower earnings growth, lower long-term earnings, lower savings, lower retirement and health benefits, greater work stress, more blow-up confrontations with colleagues and clients and investors, and more psychosomatic health problems than individuals employed at regular jobs.

For businesses requiring a lot of seed capital, it is often the venture capitalists—private investors who invest significant sums of money in early-stage companies founded by entrepreneurs—who are in it for a fast financial return. They attempt to get in on the ground floor and bring in other, later-stage investors at a higher implied (paper) valuation. Investors and media outlets who cover venture capital fixate on these implied valuations, which may or may not have anything to do with the business or its products. It helps to explain the fraught relationship between entrepreneurs and venture capitalists.

Despite the media preoccupation with venture capital, in truth, most people who start a business want no part of venture capital, which comes with many strings attached. I turned away venture capitalist (often called VC) money at several times in my career, surprised at how unappealing the terms were. VCs often want decision-making authority over business strategy. Frequently, too, they will demand a special class of shares in return for an early investment, affording them super-voting rights (again, more control) if a company goes public. If a VC gives you one million dollars for preferential shares or convertible debt, or if they install their people or their friends on your board to represent a majority of the votes for all decisions, then you are doing their bidding, not your own, nor that of the community about which you are most concerned.

Though VCs claim to "raise" sums (often huge ones) for entrepreneurs, this language is misleading: the money isn't gifted to you; it's more accurately described as a contingent loan. In many cases, accepting VC money comes with more disadvantages than benefits; most entrepreneurs I know share this view yet, in conflict with this, there's an unwritten axiom of entrepreneurship that goes like this: "if you need the money and it's on offer, take it *now*."

Entrepreneurs are by definition independent-minded: the statistics I've already noted show that most entrepreneurs start businesses because, in part, they crave autonomy. Their tendency by nature is to avoid financing models that handcuff them and deprive them of the very autonomy that motivates them.

They do, however, want what money and fame can mean for their enterprise: bigger markets, more customers, greater recognition for their work. They have ground-breaking new ideas and innovations to offer the world, and they get excited about the prospect of seeing those offerings travel as far and as widely as possible. This is why, despite everything, some entrepreneurs do eventually accept VC funding on poor terms, entering into relationships that allow them to grow, but also—because now there are funders who want returns on their investments involved—that force them to grow faster than they might actually want. It's also why many run into problems with fast-fluctuating dopamine levels.

6

ENTREPRENEURS
AND DOPAMINE

I N 2021, CARIN-ISABEL KNOOP, executive director of the Harvard Business School Case Research and Writing Group, responsible for leading the development of business case studies that train new generations of entrepreneurs and business executives, noted that business schools historically have "presented business leaders and case protagonists as unaffected by outside stressors or health issues. The classroom narratives of neutral individuals dealing with challenging problems with finesse leave little room in the conversation to discuss topics of mental health."

It may be that the psychology of entrepreneurship and its association with mental health burdens are understudied because they are complicated. In my view, the dearth of scientific research on the more particular relationship between dopamine and entrepreneurship is at least partially due to the fact that it would need to draw on several quite different fields of study: business, clinical psychology, and neuroscience. Researchers in these fields don't often speak to one another, most have not started ventures of their own so they are lacking in personal experience and may, indeed, be either oblivious or hostile to findings that come from other quarters despite a trend in universities toward promoting interdisciplinary research.

Nevertheless, a few researchers have attempted to address psychological aspects of entrepreneurship. A highly cited 1983 paper in the *Strategic Management Journal* by business school academics Norman Smith of the University of Oregon and John Miner of Georgia State University, identified what they considered to be five basic components of entrepreneurial motivation: (1) self-achievement or a desire to achieve through one's own efforts and be able to attribute any success to oneself; (2) clear feedback that measures performance; (3) a desire to innovate, to introduce creative solutions to important problems; (4) planning ahead for the future; and (5) the desire to avoid risks whenever possible.[6]

---

6 The concept of risk is historically tied to new business ventures and new business contracts in particular. The *ašipu*, priests and exorcists practicing their craft in the Tigris-Euphrates valley in Mesopotamia, conceived of risk prediction in business as early as 3200 BCE. *Ašipu* approached the problem rationally, collecting data and considering alternative routes of conduct. They formulated probabilistic concepts of profit, loss, success, and failure in new ventures. The Code of Hammurabi, a collection of 282 laws inscribed in Babylonian cuneiform on stone, later embedded these concepts of risk in the design of new business contracts. In seventeenth-century Britain, the word "risk" attained its current connotations of exposure to danger. The Crown borrowed heavily to finance its army; in times of war, it could default on those debts, leaving creditors holding the bag. When the Bank of England became a private institution in 1694, it was endowed with the power to raise money for the government and other borrowers by issuing bonds and calculating risk dividends and repayment

I have a quarrel with the last point. It's true that smart entrepreneurs avoid unnecessary risks but, in my experience, taking risks is part of the job of an entrepreneur, and part of the thrill of the job. In fact, the job is all about *managing* what some entrepreneurs refer to as "healthy risk." And many entrepreneurs, in negotiations with lenders, take excessive, irrational financial risks and fall into a debt spiral in ever-more desperate attempts to finance their ventures. Some fail; some manage to succeed. Understanding entrepreneurs requires understanding risk and the gradient of risk. All competitive contact sports, by analogy, carry some level of risk. Like the boxer (I was an amateur-level boxer during my early thirties) the entrepreneur manages the risk inside the four corners of the ring, donning head protection, taking pains to throw selective and targeted punches and to "never rush the technique."

* * *

Those five components of entrepreneurial motivation first observed by researchers Smith and Miner are pieces of the puzzle but they don't really get at the fundamental dopamine-induced and sometimes dopamine-dysregulated impulses and demands of entrepreneurship. Where do the observable or self-reported traits of entrepreneurs

---

terms. Our modern global finance system understands risk as natural and necessary for pursuing a future-oriented goal. The banking system formally adopted this concept by fashioning structured contingent business loans and creating lines of credit based on an assessment of the likelihood of repayment.

come from? What explains the commonalities, individualities, risk mentalities, and idiosyncratic obsessions of the people I have interacted with in the start-up, investor, and business worlds? Those are the questions that intrigue me and require investigation to make sense of the strengths but also the frailties of the entrepreneurial mind.

No researchers that I know of are experts in all the neuroscientific underpinnings of entrepreneurial behaviour. Perhaps you need to be an entrepreneur to fully understand the motives, conflicts, impulses, and reactions that spur their sometimes inexplicable, seemingly irrational behaviour. Every start-up founder I've met or considered investing in will tell you that the only way to appreciate the continual peaks and valleys of a new business venture is to start one yourself.

Craig Hudson, the dopamine researcher and entrepreneur, told me that "when it comes to real dopamine science and entrepreneurship, and understanding that connectivity, nobody talks about this, and they certainly don't understand it in business schools." Craig knew what he was talking about.

When I started looking in the Google Scholar database in the summer of 2021, I discovered just thirty-six academic papers on dopamine and personality. Knowing how dopamine coats certain events and experiences with salience, encoding their importance to us, and also knowing how crucial dopamine is to the perception of and tolerance for risk, I was looking for evidence to test my hypothesis that dopamine is a big part of what makes an entrepreneur an entrepreneur. My premise was that entrepreneurialism is an inherently dopaminergic activity, which is to say that all entrepreneurs share a propensity to be driven, or to suffer, far more than the average, by dopamine release and flux. And many struggle, I have seen this repeatedly, with the vicissitudes that come from the ebb and flow of dopamine secretion.

The entrepreneurial environment is difficult and competitive. It requires long hours that eat into sleep and family time. It requires imagination, commitment, and the kind of cognitive flexibility that most of us do not have—the capacity to make quick decisions at times but, at other times, the need to curb one's natural impulses and do nothing. The energy, speed, and decisiveness that entrepreneurs require are traits born of dopamine. Recalling the work of my father and his colleagues about the concept of dopamine "high state," it seemed to me that the entrepreneurial life requires enormous amounts of dopamine bursts that demand discipline to navigate. Dopamine accelerates so it helps with quick decisions. Probably it accounts for the "wild spirits" and "fiery souls" first noted by the economist Schumpeter.

It also accounts for why failure is a big part of entrepreneurship. A significant majority of entrepreneurs periodically fail, and many on a grand scale. Across industrialized countries, it is generally the case that roughly 20 percent of new businesses fail in their first year, two thirds fail within the first six years, and, typically, only 25 percent last more than five years. What is it about the ones in this last category—why do they survive as long as they do? One reason relates to denial. More than half of all entrepreneurs continue to invest their own money into their ventures even after receiving sound advice to cease operations. Approximately 30 percent will persist even after their ventures are declared failures.

Why do they persist? It may be a specific form of entrepreneurial delusion, that they can manage the chaos of the universe sufficiently to mark, through hard work, an indelible dent in its design. Or it may be stubbornness. Being stubborn is part of succeeding as an entrepreneur.

Reviewing the literature, I learned that scientists have been accumulating evidence since the mid-1990s that some of the dopamine receptors cloned in my father's lab are, in fact, elevated in the brains of entrepreneurs. These are the ones related to sensation-seeking. Studies also show that the tendency to want to be an entrepreneur is heritable and that people with tendencies toward sensation-seeking and people with entrepreneurial inclinations share similar dopamine-related genes.

A 2020 paper in the journal *Cortex* by Alexandra Touroutoglou and colleagues of Massachusetts General Hospital and Harvard Medical School addresses the related personality traits of tenacity, grit, and perseverance in the face of obstacles. The paper is entitled "The Tenacious Brain: How the Anterior Mid-Cingulate Contributes to Achieving Goals." The anterior mid-cingulate is a structure in the front part of the brain that is richly served by dopamine neurons so it is safe to assume that dopamine contributes to the vital-to-success entrepreneurial trait of tenacity.

And indeed, entrepreneurs are tenacious about taking risks. In 2016, Robb Rutledge at University College, London, published a study that shed some light on this possibility. He asked healthy adult volunteers to perform a gambling task—once after taking a dopamine-like medication and once after taking a placebo. The task involved choosing between safe and risky options that could cause participants to gain or lose money. They could choose between getting a small reward (or suffering a small loss) and the chance of getting a large reward (or suffering a large loss). The results showed that, while on dopamine, the study participants, blinded as to the nature of the study's thesis, took significantly more risks than they did on the placebo.

In 2010, researcher Nicos Nicolaou at the University of Cyprus and his colleague Scott Shane, then at Case Western Reserve University, discovered an important genetic association between dopamine and entrepreneurship. Based on prior observations that genes associated with ADHD were prevalent among entrepreneurs, the researchers studied a sample of 1,335 individuals from the United Kingdom who had been diagnosed with ADHD. They found that their DNA configurations were significantly associated with choosing to become an entrepreneur. ADHD has long been known to be associated with dopamine.

In a larger twin study that same year, Nicolaou and colleagues showed that there was a clear (though not overwhelming) genetic variation that maps to two of what psychologists sometimes call the "Big Five" personality traits: extraversion and openness to experience. (The other three are conscientiousness, agreeableness, and neuroticism.) Some psychologists believe this taxonomy can help them understand the relationship between different personalities and different patterns of behaviour. In this study, researchers found that the two traits they had mapped tended to distinguish self-employed people—a rough proxy for entrepreneurship—from those who work for others. The authors noted that we are unlikely to ever find entrepreneurship-specific genes, but that genes may influence a tendency toward needing to be independent in one's work.

Manic or hypomanic personality is a concept I found described in more than 1,700 peer-reviewed scientific papers dating back to the mid-1980s. Hypomania is a period of intense, elevated energy and mood. It is associated with such traits as impulsivity, elevated risk-taking, ambition, overconfidence, extraversion, tenacity, and—something I'd seen all too often among entrepreneurs of all types—a relative lack of respect for social norms. Although the exact mechanisms in the brain that are involved in hypomania are not fully understood, we do know that hypomania sometimes follows after dopamine-replacement therapy in people with Parkinson's. It stands to reason, then, that hypomanic tendencies are fuelled, at least to some extent, by dopamine. And if that's the case, it seems plausible that there may be some correlation between hypomania and entrepreneurship.

That was the exact hypothesis that Helen Pushkarskaya of the Yale department of psychiatry and her colleagues at the Max Planck Institute and at Cornell University set out to test recently. They studied the association of hypomanic tendencies with entrepreneurial activities in three different populations. Their hunch was borne out (though, at the time of writing, their findings were in pre-publication peer review). "We report a robust positive association of [hypomania] with several measures of entrepreneurial intent, behavior, and success," the researchers wrote. They found that hypomanic tendencies, such as mood volatility, were most elevated in people actively in the process of starting a new business—that is, in nascent entrepreneurs. "This may reflect a particular ecological fit between individual characteristics associated with [hypomania] and unique demands of [an] entrepreneurial lifestyle," they wrote, "but highlights the psychological vulnerability of entrepreneurs, especially under conditions of stress."

In a seminal 1986 paper published in the *Journal of Abnormal Psychology*, Mark Eckblad and Loren Chapman of the University of Wisconsin-Madison tested 1,519 undergraduate students on a scientifically validated hypomanic personality scale score, and found that high scores were significantly associated with subsequent bipolar disorder. No fewer maladies than anxiety, depression, ADHD, addiction, and bipolar disorder appear to be risks for entrepreneurs, and these mental health conditions all involve dopamine. It is not entirely clear at this stage of investigation if people with dopamine-related inherent tendencies are more likely to become entrepreneurs, or if becoming an entrepreneur predisposes you to these conditions.

It sounds strange to think that scientific investigators are looking for genes that determine what field of work you will enter. But as my scientist father taught me, nothing is straightforwardly due to either nature or nurture; it's always a matter of both.

Many entrepreneurs, I have hypothesized, through a combination of nature and nurture, are particularly sensitive to dopamine. That sensitivity may be what attracts them to entrepreneurship in the first place. The opposite is also true. The entrepreneurial life can wreak havoc on a person's dopamine regulation. The highs are extremely high and addictive. The lows can be devastating. This combination of factors accounts for at least some of the unique vulnerability of a large subset of entrepreneurs: as a group, they may not just take ordinary risks, they may become foolhardy; they may not just take pleasure in their accomplishments but rather they become addicted to the "high" that success brings.

7

THE TORMENTS OF ENTREPRENEURS

WITH THE COMMERCIALIZATION OF the World Wide Web after 1992, a new persona was thrust upon the world: the Internet entrepreneur. Back then, the Internet was much smaller than it is today; there were only a few websites that attracted many visitors with any frequency. Like many others making their first online forays, I spent a fair bit of time surfing America Online (or AOL) chat groups. In my case, it was to share stories of my social anxiety and shyness. As the saying goes, "a burden shared is a burden halved," and since there were so many listeners online and it was all anonymous, my burden was considerably lightened.

Also, back then and still to a small extent today, the wealthiest class of Internet entrepreneurs were domain-name buyers and sellers, people who snapped up domains like apple.com and quickly flipped the digital real estate to large corporations, like Apple Inc., for millions of dollars.

Many early domainers I got to know well later became pioneers in brand new business fields such as cyber-security, e-commerce, online job search, and advertising technology; this was partly because, through natural search traffic coming to their sites from across the world, they could readily convert their one-word business domains, like resume.com, into monetizable businesses by placing third-party ads on related content—for example, how best to write a professional business résumé—and charging advertisers a monthly fee for access to the audience. This is the backbone revenue model of many early Internet successes, like booking.com, the Dutch online travel agency launched in 1996. Outside of the offices of venture capital firms, which often deride domainers as lazy and stupid, many former domainers are revered by operators in diverse business sectors for their tenacity and innovation.

Which brings me to a guy who I will call Roman. Roman was a good friend from the business community and in 2014, he asked me for a favour. Two former colleagues of mine who had once been domainers had founded several ventures, one of which was among the top domain name and advertising technology conference events, held annually across the world, and frequently hosted in Las Vegas. Roman asked to attend and, thinking this would be a great entrepreneurial networking opportunity for him, I got him an invitation.

To get Roman into this Vegas event, which was crowded with Internet investors, I had vouched for Roman to a domainer friend, which I did in good conscience. Unfortunately, a few days into the conference, I got a text from one of my former colleagues saying that Roman had been kicked out.

"I won't call the police since he's your guy," he went on. "But he can't step foot in our conference or meet-ups in Vegas ever again." "Roman," he said, "was on coke, or more likely meth," Roman had turned violent; the domainer, who had played striker for a competitive soccer club earlier in his life, had had to literally pick Roman up and boot him out of the pub.

That was the first time I'd heard about coke and meth use among entrepreneurs. Now, it seems that the topic comes up at least once a week.

Wanting to better understand Roman's behaviour, I called Sean Fogler, my oldest friend; we grew up on the same street in Toronto. Sean was working as an anaesthesiologist in downtown Philadelphia, and so he knew a lot about dopamine-firing addictive drugs like cocaine and meth. Sean asked me to give him some background to the Vegas incident, and he then told me that he was of the view that crystal meth, which can trigger impulsive, violent behaviour, was the likely culprit.

I remember being impressed by Sean's encyclopaedic knowledge of the minutiae of how people act when they are doped up, and the ease with which he could communicate these facts and details. Sean was himself an entrepreneur: an energetic polymath talented in many fields. Years before all this, he had paused his practice of medicine to spend two years as a trader on Wall Street, one of several mini sabbaticals and detours he took to accommodate creative and entrepreneurial ambitions. (Another of these creative outlets was DJ'ing; he was asked to play at many clubs across America: New York City, Miami, and Las Vegas.)

About four months later, Sean went MIA. His phone mailbox was full, unable to take messages, and nobody, including a mutual friend from childhood, then living in Houston, had any clue as to his whereabouts. This silence continued for three months, during which I periodically received calls from investors and casual friends we had in common who wanted to know where Sean was. The last time I'd seen Sean was in Philadelphia, at a posh dinner for investors in the private downstairs dining room at Morimoto restaurant, where he had organized a gathering on my behalf.

Eventually, Sean called me. For the last four months, he said, he had been in a recovery clinic in Delray Beach, Florida (the recovery capital of America), and in the back-to-nature recovery escape he was calling me from in Kentucky. We could only speak for a short time, he said: the administrators frowned on smartphone usage for people in recovery. A smartphone, Sean explained, can be an "enabler" of unhealthy behaviours, as is social media.

Everything about Sean's scenario was bewildering to me. Prior to that call, I had no idea that Sean was addicted to cocaine. The added sting was that his police mugshot was featured in Philadelphia newspapers that week. He had been picked up by the cops for writing a handful of prescriptions to another person struggling with addiction.

In the years since, it has been Sean, through his slow, steady climb from out under the weight of addiction and the US criminal justice system, who taught me about how dopamine and addiction work in real life, outside of the laboratory and peer-reviewed research. I learned over time that Sean had struggled with post-traumatic stress disorder (PTSD) originating in childhood traumas and retriggered by his presence at the Twin Towers on September 11, 2001, when he was working on Wall Street. The PTSD was the underlying cause of his addiction.

By the time of his arrest, Sean was in recovery and in group therapy. He was sentenced, in Montgomery County Court, to five years' probation after pleading guilty to charges of acquiring controlled substances by fraud.

Sean is now one of the best-known people in recovery in the United States, speaking about addiction among physicians. He educates and trains police and sheriffs across Pennsylvania and the United States about how to help sufferers from addiction recover and find hope instead of jail.

* * *

Drug addiction among high performers of all types is not new. The hedonistic treadmill, for an entrepreneur and any breaker of social norms, is not easy to resist. Life's demands and stresses wear one down. The father of modern American surgery, William Halsted of Johns Hopkins University Hospital, was addicted to cocaine and morphine. Sigmund Freud, like Halsted, was addicted to cocaine, yet continued to treat patients and to enrich psychology, literature, and modern cultural traditions through his writing.

The timing and clinical signs and symptoms of drug addiction differ for each drug and for each person. They depend on drug dosage, the timing and speed of drug intake, whether the drug is inhaled or taken by mouth or injected, the frequency of drug usage, the number of days or months or years that the drug has been used, and the individual metabolisms of different people. Despite the large variety of potentially addictive compounds and behaviours (which include alcohol and nicotine as well as harder drugs, and a range of habits such as gambling), there is one common pathway to addiction: the dopamine receptors that modulate risk and reward, dopamine D4 and dopamine D2, respectively.

The release of dopamine from neuron terminals has been studied in several types of addiction. When amphetamines or cocaine are injected into a person's vein, the drugs almost immediately cause a release of dopamine from dopamine terminals, which is experienced as pleasure. Drugs that act rapidly, such as cocaine and especially "crack" cocaine, cause a correspondingly swift release of dopamine, which can create intensely pleasurable feelings and a more severe addiction than drugs that take time to achieve their effect. That the common brain pathway for addictions is the dopamine pathway helps to explain why dopamine-sensitive entrepreneurs are particularly vulnerable to addiction.

Why, we could ask, if addiction is so dangerous to our species, has evolution allowed addictions to plague us? As in Chinese philosophy, there is a yin and yang to addiction. In her 2021 book *Dopamine Nation*, psychiatrist Anna Lembke of Stanford University explores both the pleasure aspect of dopamine and the counterproductive behaviour of patients suffering from dopamine-induced pleasure-seeking addictions. She suggested to me that having an addictive personality might, in fact, hold positive adaptive value; it might have helped our species succeed. An authority on addiction science in addition to her work in psychiatry, Lembke told me that some people are clearly more vulnerable to addictions than others. Her view is that addictive personalities are tenacious, not only in their pursuit of their drug of choice, but also in their pursuit of their mission in life. In Darwinian terms, "this ability to work harder and travel further to get a higher and better drug of choice was highly adaptive. It's endemic, and, in my view, a highly adaptive feature," she said.

Her observation is consistent with our earlier discussion of the sometimes positive repercussions of impulsivity, aggression, and even delusions. Nevertheless, it shook me because tenacious people working harder and travelling further pretty much describes everyone I preferred to surround myself with in the entrepreneurial world. That addiction has adaptive value might be plausible at a societal level, but it is disturbing at an individual level.

* * *

Dopamine is a versatile chemical. It plays an important role in addiction and is implicated in many other mental health conditions. It is central to something I mentioned at the outset of this chapter: the onset and development of anxiety. The connection between dopamine and anxiety is of more than academic interest to me. I was nicknamed "neurotic Neil" by my classmates and campmates throughout school. I have another nickname, "two-gear," for you can generally find me in very high or very low states of anxiety.

85

The experience of anxiety, at heart, is a distressing apprehension of what *might* happen. It is a response to events that represent potential threats. Anxiety sometimes shows itself as preoccupation, rumination, rapid heartbeat, tremor, sweating, confusion, flushing, dizziness, and fear. Dopamine interacts with its neurotransmitter colleagues, the adrenergic, cholinergic, glutamatergic and GABAergic, opioidergic, cannabinoid, and histaminergic systems, to modulate anxiety and the behavioural responses (fight or flight) that anxiety evokes. If dopamine becomes dysregulated, a person can wind up in trouble, falling prey to anxieties they cannot effectively manage.

We all, as entrepreneurs, experience anxiety in its several forms. Some entrepreneurs who need to travel and who repeatedly leave home experience separation anxiety. This is a term associated with toddlers missing their mothers but separation anxiety persists throughout life and surfaces whenever we are separated from people or objects that function as security blankets.

Another common form of entrepreneurial anxiety is social anxiety—the fear of meeting new people, and the fear of speaking in public. This is paradoxical because entrepreneurs are always meeting new people and very often need to be in the public eye. Social anxiety affects individuals who have very high expectations of themselves and are, therefore, chronically afraid of not being able to live up to their own high standards. Other forms of anxiety are obsessions, phobias, tics, nail biting, and PTSD, all very commonplace. Recent findings confirm the fact that anxieties arise, at least in part, from excessive dopamine neurotransmission.

Anxiety and ADHD are closely related, and ADHD is probably the condition that is most widely understood to be implicated in entrepreneurialism. In the circles I travel in, both around the university and in the start-up community, hypomania and ADHD are increasingly referred to as "CEO disease." In some circles, ADHD and what my friends call "overactive brain syndrome" are more or less synonyms for entrepreneurship.

I have known a handful of highly successful and frenetic entrepreneurs who told me they suffered from ADHD, or had been so diagnosed at a certain period in their life. And we have all seen ADHD-like behaviour in big-name entrepreneurs such as Tesla and SpaceX founder Elon Musk, who has openly mocked other entrepreneurs who work humdrum, regular business hours. Musk didn't learn he had ADHD until he was in his thirties and, in a TV interview, he described the condition as akin to intense impulsivity.

Anxiety and depression are two of the most common psychiatric illnesses and they are closely linked. As we saw in the first chapter on suicide, many entrepreneurs suffer from major depression. Again, most ventures fail, and failure produces psychological pain. The end of a business and bankruptcy inevitably constitutes a significant loss for the founder, but what most people would consider a successful "exit" can also cause distress.[7] The company you founded is very much your progeny; you suffer when it is gone and when someone else steps in to take your place as its leader.

---

7 Sherry Walling, a clinical psychologist and writer on entrepreneurship and its discontents, told me that entrepreneurs can be devastated following an exit, resulting in serious depression. Yet they can learn, with time, to feel gratitude rather than sorrow on reaching this next stage in their lives. As Walling puts it, the entrepreneur can reframe an event such as an exit or resignation as an arrival rather than a departure.

Most exits are complicated because most founders are trapped after they sell through earn-out provisions and other tie-ups. There is even a recognized condition called "success depression." Success always has strings attached and those strings can drag down your mood. Success always brings added responsibilities and heightens social expectations or entrepreneurial expectations of a repeat success, which many find weighs them down—less free time, more deadlines, more people to please.

When a person is depressed, dopamine neurotransmission is reduced. This could result from diminished dopamine release from presynaptic neurons or changes in postsynaptic receptor numbers or from super-sensitivity to dopamine fluctuations. Some antidepressants act directly through dopamine, but most current antidepression treatments do not directly enhance dopamine neurotransmission (many do so indirectly).

As we saw in the opening chapter, suicide, often the result of untreated depression, is much too prevalent among entrepreneurs. Far too many founders—accomplished, self-made people remarkable in their outward achievements—decide to take their lives. And not only entrepreneurs, of course, but super creatives in all forms of endeavour, including Robin Williams, Kurt Cobain, Alan Turing, Virginia Woolf, Sylvia Plath, and Hunter S. Thompson. There are always reasons, but the reasons never seem proportionate to the final, irreversible act.

Dr. Michael Freeman, the University of California at San Francisco professor of psychiatry who has done extensive research into mental illness and entrepreneurship, is a renowned entrepreneur in his own right, having started more than ten for-profit and not-for-profit ventures. He is frequently called upon to counsel grieving families in the aftermath of a premature death—usually a suicide—of a young entrepreneur.

"I have this unique experience of being an entrepreneur, understanding mental health, and going on the same journey as everybody that I'm trying to understand," said Freeman. "These were kids who were 'touched with fire.'" The phrase comes from psychologist Kay Redfield Jamison's 1996 classic, *Touched with Fire: Manic-Depressive Illness and the Artistic Temperament*, a popular book about the possible links between bipolar disorder and creativity. Bipolar people are drawn to entrepreneurship, said Freeman, and entrepreneurship, with its extreme highs and lows, is itself almost a bipolar pursuit: "It takes a certain type to be drawn to that." Thanks in part to the 2022 book, *Burn Rate*, by Andy Dunn, the co-founder and former CEO of the men's clothing company Bonobos bought by Walmart in 2017, the link between bipolarity and entrepreneurship—Andy Dunn's long-held secret—has been unmasked. Dunn's condition is commonplace among entrepreneurs; he is part of the 11 percent of entrepreneurs (compared to just 4.4 percent of US adults) who suffer from bipolar disorder.

* * *

If entrepreneurs, as a class, are prone to bipolar disorder, depression, anxiety, ADHD, mania, grandiose delusions, among other ills, does that mean they suffer from official and, thus, treatable conditions?

It is not as simple a question as it may sound. Making a firm diagnosis of any specific illness is difficult in psychiatry. There are no confirmatory blood tests or X-rays for psychiatric illnesses; diagnoses are made on the basis of a person's reported symptoms—and what counts as a symptom or what a person experiences as unusually distressing is not fixed. Nor are society's norms and standards for behaviour and mental illness. A level of stress that many people might find debilitating may be entirely normal for an Olympic-level athlete; an experienced psychiatrist will assess and treat these two extremes differently.

The fluidity of our concepts of mental illness is reflected in the fact that the criteria for a diagnosis, and sometimes even for what counts as an illness at all, keep changing. The Diagnostic and Statistical Manual of Mental Disorders (often just referred to as the DSM) is the primary text for classifying mental illnesses in North America. It is updated every few years; every time a new edition is released, practicing psychiatrists and psychologists and other therapists need to catch up, as some illnesses will have been removed and others added, and still others will have had their diagnostic criteria revised.

Ian and Joel Gold, the brothers who wrote *Suspicious Minds: How Culture Shapes Madness*, argue that the medical consensus that delusions are manifestations of some sort of brain dysfunction is reductive, and mistaken. Our brains don't exist in isolation from the world, spinning delusions out of a vacuum, they argue. We are part of the socio-cultural world around us. The causes of delusions, they contend, are circular: an experience will influence our dopamine levels which, in turn, influence the responses we elicit from others and the circumstances that befall us.

Although they haven't looked at entrepreneurship specifically, Ian told me that a dopamine-sensitive entrepreneur may be an example of the kind of person who would exhibit a wide variety of behaviours that casual observers would glibly call "crazy." They may tear themselves apart over whether or not to accept certain investments, or whether or not to trust their co-founders; they may stubbornly refuse to share information about their inventions or see others plotting to undermine their businesses. In other contexts, such behaviours may seem pathological. In an entrepreneurial environment, they can be adaptive and understood as rational.

Delusions are sometimes defined as a person losing touch with reality. Another way of saying this is that delusions are what happens when you perceive reality very differently than do the people around you. "Psychosis," said Ian, "is the price we pay for having a social world." Entrepreneurial grandiosity and entrepreneurial paranoia depend partly on neurochemicals but also on the interactions that entrepreneurs have with their social world. Ian believes that such entrepreneurs manifest "a *healthy psychosis* to which we owe a debt."

8

ENTREPRENEURS AND THE BIG DIVIDE

Y FRIEND, ALEXANDER MOSA, now a medical student at McMaster Medical School, is an entrepreneur. He completed an undergraduate degree in ancient history at the University of Toronto, then organized an international science team to discover a cure for Hepatitis C, from which his architect and entrepreneur father had died at fifty-eight. Alex followed that up by developing a new drug for Hepatitis C while completing a doctorate in virology, and, at the same time, building and selling a biomedical engineering company. He was, at this point, in his mid-twenties.

Alex embodies the tenacious entrepreneurial spirit. Many years ago, I helped him with due diligence and background checks on the investors we considered might be helpful to his ventures. As we worked, we would talk, quite often, about an ancient Roman philosopher named Seneca. Seneca (who lived from 4 BCE to 65 CE) was the leading Stoic philosopher of his time; his teachings focused on living a life of virtue. An entrepreneur himself, Seneca, as a playwright, wrote eight tragedies plus the first and only Roman textbook on physics. His writings stress that what fundamentally matters in entrepreneurial life is hard work on behalf of one's community. Alex took this counsel very much to heart. Discipline, self-control, and ridding yourself of negative emotions like anger and envy are all essential to a good life, the Stoics say. So, too, is being judicious with your time, prudent about the friends and colleagues with whom you choose to spend your time, and selective about the books you read. The ideal is to be steered throughout life by altruism, driven to action by the ambition to contribute to the prosperity and well-being of your community. Alex is far from the only entrepreneur I know who has been inspired by Seneca. For many years, Stoic values prevailed in the entrepreneurial world. Less so today.

The shift away from Stoic values often is described by entrepreneurs as an embrace of a different school of philosophy: Epicureanism, or the view that the goal of life is attaining happiness. It's a widely misunderstood position: the word "epicure," denoting a follower of the Greek philosopher Epicurus, has come to mean someone who revels in self-indulgence and pleasure. But that isn't what Epicurus meant by happiness. He argued that happiness is best understood as the absence of pain and distress. For him, a well-lived life was one free of anxiety, one in which a person accepts the inevitable, takes the ups and downs and injustices of life with equanimity. In other words, you need to roll with (and to expect) frequent punches.

Despite this, modern dictionaries, such as Collins and Webster's, define an Epicurean simply as someone fond of luxury, gourmet food, or indulgence; and so, for many entrepreneurs, especially since 2008 (more on this later), Epicureanism has come to mean making money, and making it fast, a form of hedonism. The shift towards this way of thinking has not been subtle: "Epicure" has risen in popularity as a name for corporate finance and venture capital firms in major investment hubs in the United States, Qatar, France, India, and Australia. "Epicurean" was the name of a new AI-driven bot that invested in cryptocurrencies (another popular bot-investor in crypto was named "Stoic").

* * *

It is natural that there are all kinds of entrepreneurs, just as there are all kinds of people. The entrepreneurial condition is far more complicated than any categories we can develop for it, but I do find it useful to divide entrepreneurs into two distinct groups, the hedonists and the Stoics. This is, of course, an oversimplification: I'm arbitrarily dividing what is really a spectrum into two opposing parts. However, there do exist hedonists, the "fast money guys," who are corrupting the genuine good in entrepreneurialism (and, yes, they are mostly guys). In the main, they are investors who have given innovation a bad name and who helped steer us toward the selfish entrepreneurialism increasingly prevalent in the community.

What do I mean by fast-money guys?

Back in the autumn of 2013, I found myself at the Toronto Sheraton Hotel's banquet hall. White block letters scrolled down a wall-sized flat-screen TV, spelling out the names of the individuals who had been selected to judge a contest that was then called "The Next 36," an annual competition for new entrepreneurial talent in Canada. The event was sponsored by the nation's top financial institutions and philanthropists. I was one of the judges.

The theme for that year was mobile technology. I had been investing in mobile health technology since 2007 so I was interested, and maybe a little envious, too. The young winners would win acclaim and be able to secure funding to start new mobile tech ventures almost immediately.

I looked around awkwardly, one hand fidgeting in my pocket, the other hand clutching pre-dinner hors d'oeuvres. As judges and contestants and guests mingled, I tried to think of conversation-starters.

"Hey, how was Florida this year?" I asked a confident-looking man walking toward me in a purple-chequered blazer and sandals. He looked familiar—I'd met him the year before, at a dinner party held in a grand white house in the gated, white-sand community of Vero Beach, Florida. He had beamed with pride, or so I recalled, when I had asked him that night about his eye-catching watch. I remembered trying, on a deck chair by a pool, to appear as if I'd recognized the watchmaker he named. I recalled his wife as charming; she'd run a charity that involved childhood education. But I had been preoccupied with his watch. It seemed enormous to me—oddly oversized and ill-suited to his slender frame. I was learning that BTWs—big thick watches—are popular among hedonists in the modern investor community. They are conspicuous by design, worn to telegraph the wealth and authority of the wearer.

The purple-blazer man looked puzzled when I asked him about Vero Beach. "Veeeroh?" he shouted above the cocktail din. "You're thinking of that guy, the MC, there." At this point I realized I had mis-remembered, confusing this man with the person I'd met last year, someone altogether different. Such confusion is common for me since I find social gatherings stressful.

Purple-blazer guy, it turns out, was TV-level famous, one of the "Dragons" on the long-running show "Dragon's Den," Canada's analogue to "The Shark Tank." "Dragon's Den" and "The Shark Tank" shared a lead character, Kevin O'Leary. He is both a Dragon and a Shark, an over-the-top character who calls himself "Mr. Wonderful" and whose billionaire status has been challenged in the Canadian financial press. Big thick watch guy from Vero Beach was, as purple blazer noted, the master of ceremonies for the evening. It turned out that BTW guy, in addition to being the MC, was a former business partner of Mr. Wonderful.

That is the world of the fast-money guys. As should be evident by this point, it also runs on dopamine.

I saw someone else I sort of knew at the Toronto Sheraton that evening: John, who later founded a leading Canadian investment fund that sponsors contrarian business ideas and polymath founders. I remembered that John had known some people who had put in an early offer to buy half of one of my ventures. His name was always mentioned as a sort of investor sage, so I introduced myself to him that night.

"Hey, great to see you," John said. He had an easy smile that encouraged confidences.

"I'm not feeling so comfortable here," I told him.

"Why?"

"I never feel comfortable around really successful founder-type people."

"Don't worry, Neil," he told me. "Almost nobody here is, in all probability, an entrepreneur."

That was unexpected. We got into a conversation and I asked him, "What variable, if any, predicts entrepreneurial success?"

What he told me was still more unexpected. His answer had nothing to do with education, or wealth, or intelligence, or even networking—none of the advantages that are usually invoked to explain unusual levels of achievement. The secret to entrepreneurial success, he said, was Mom and Dad.

In his thirty years of investing, John explained, he had learned that what distinguished entrepreneurs who flourished from those who didn't was a quality, cultivated with the help of parents, of something like determination or persistence—a stick-to-it-iveness. It was the capacity to keep going in the face of scepticism, and it was something that had been instilled in them, usually when young. I've since seen research that supports the notion that entrepreneurial behaviour is modelled on either parents or empathic mentors.

I told him about my mother, fleeing from the Nazis as a child, and her commitment to understanding the ways psychiatric illness differs in men and women, an idea that was heresy at the time she first wrote about it. And then I told him about my father, his pursuit of dopamine receptors, and the stories he told me about how he needed to rely on donations from individual families affected by mental illness, in addition to grants from agencies such as the US National Institutes of Health, to fund his research. During the

1960s, my father had applied to a top US national science funding agency for support of his early research into dopamine; one peer reviewer, tenured at an Ivy League university, wrote just three words on his grant application: "This is shit." But my father had another source of funds. Grateful families of patients who had benefitted from his discoveries gave life-saving donations to his lab.

"Your Dad is an entrepreneur. Dopamine. Classic, I love it," John told me.

John's definition of an entrepreneur was tuned to entrepreneurs in the Stoic tradition, motivated far less by fame or wealth or self-aggrandizement, and far more by the prospect of solving important problems and of creating something useful for one's community. True entrepreneurs in the Stoic tradition don't like to talk about valuations and market caps, and they don't wear big watches. They consider venture capitalists, with important exceptions, to be vultures, self-styled masters of the investment universe.

My emerging hypothesis was that the fast-money guys see their ventures as projects in self-aggrandizement: their dopamine attaches to the rewards that money brings, to the wielding of power, to winning out over competitors. Classical or Stoic entrepreneurs also seek self-fulfillment, but of a different sort. Their dopamine attaches to the satisfaction of creating things, finding solutions, and impacting their communities for the better. I sometimes call the latter group "value-oriented" entrepreneurs to emphasize that they have both deeply held values and a focus on creating value.

Put another way, value-oriented entrepreneurs are motivated by the Japanese concept of *ikigai*: do what you love, what you're good at, what will earn you a livelihood, but, most important, do what will be truly useful to your community or your world. Entrepreneurs driven by *ikigai*—Ray Kroc who started McDonald's System, Inc., giving birth to the McDonald's Corporation, designer and philanthropist Ralph Lauren, chef and TV host Anthony Bourdain, or the late actress-turned-entrepreneur Debbie Reynolds—are wild spirits, to return to Schumpeter's term. These are individuals who take extreme risks, care deeply about impact and innovation, and, in the end, are the people who are responsible for dramatic changes in our societies, and the economic growth that ensues. And this is where they find their dopamine rushes: in the satisfaction of solving the problems they set out to tackle.

Still another concept that gets to the heart of the value-oriented entrepreneur is mission. In a 2022 issue of the *Journal of Business Venturing Insights*, Rai Siddhant Sinha, a researcher at the Indian Institute of Management, argues that entrepreneurs with an unbending mission treat their ventures as their offspring and form passionate, parental attachments to them. They are, he writes, psychologically invested in ensuring the right birth, nurturing, grooming, and "upbringing" for their businesses.

It is the value-oriented, *ikigai*-oriented, mission-oriented entrepreneur that Schumpeter identified as the fuel behind capitalism—the source of all material innovation, the vital force driving a capitalist economy. He spoke of impact-driven entrepreneurs and used the word *Unternehmergeist*, German for "entrepreneur-spirit," to capture this concept. Roughly, it means "the doing of new things or the doing, in a new way, of things already being done." He attributed this ability to tenacity of spirit.

* * *

Despite their very different propensities, personalities, and gratifications, the two groups of men and women I see in entrepreneurialism, hedonists and Stoics alike, are all subject to stresses and, statistically, much more likely to see failure than success. Even if they appear successful—enjoying year-over-year revenue growth, or celebrated in the media—there can be tension behind the scenes. And when failure objectively happens—say, a new product fizzles, cash dwindles, or a formerly exclusive supplier starts servicing the firm's competitors—it becomes difficult. It is harrowing to take failure philosophically, to stay measured, in the moment, and to know, intellectually, that randomness and luck can boost or derail fortunes. That said, hedonistic entrepreneurs may be able to take failure better than their value-oriented counterparts who, as a group, seem more sensitive or more reactive to the ups and downs of dopamine levels. One could ask "why"? Research doesn't provide the answer just yet, but I suspect that, when they were young and impressionable, memorable experiences shaped the development of their personalities and behavioural tendencies in this direction.

Hedonistic entrepreneurs or investors, on the other hand, consider themselves very smart and tend to attribute failure to the fault of others, or external causes. One of the advantages of being in it for yourself is that you become good at taking care of yourself and are prone to escape from defeat relatively unscathed. I am not especially concerned about their fate. If their businesses fail, they know how to shrug off the disappointment and go on to the next venture.

I *am* worried about the value-oriented entrepreneurs whose work, if successful, will benefit the communities in which they live, but whose failures are experienced as disasters. Value-oriented entrepreneurs tend to be far more invested, emotionally and financially, in the outcome of their missions, which may be relatively more difficult and take longer to achieve. They feel a high degree of personal responsibility for everything they do and blame themselves and their decisions for their failures. Defeat is seen as a product of personal deficiency. They are also more sensitive to others and fear letting people down. This combination of accountability and sensitivity amounts to a greater degree of vulnerability that leads pretty directly to heightened anxiety, sleep impairment, self-criticism, depression, addiction, and worse.

There appears to be a physiological basis to differing responses to failure. As mentioned earlier, not everyone is exposed to the same speed and flow of dopamine, and not everyone responds to dopamine in the same way. Some will develop a tolerance for the spikes of dopamine that accompany stress. Others have an opposite response, what's described in neuroscience as "dopamine sensitization." In these individuals, repeated intermittent stimulation by dopamine produces not tolerance but a progressive sensitization that eventually precipitates lasting psychological symptoms. As a result of this sensitization to dopamine transmission, relatively neutral events can gain an out-of-proportion significance, sometimes to shattering effect.

I have long wondered why some entrepreneurs succumb to the negative effects of stress and the inevitable surges of dopamine while others weather them well. Dopamine sensitization would appear to explain it. While both groups of entrepreneurs are driven by dopamine, those in the hedonist camp seem to adapt relatively easily to dopamine's fast and successive releases, developing a saving tolerance to the spikes. Value-oriented entrepreneurs seem to have a harder time dealing with successive dopamine bursts. They are more likely to become overtly symptomatic and fall into chronic depression or persistent anxiety.

This creates a double vulnerability in many value-oriented entrepreneurs. Their belief system, with its high ideals, powerful sense of mission, and strong sense of accountability and personal responsibility, renders them relatively more sensitive to stress and failure. Their brain chemistry, with its increased sensitization to successive stress-related dopamine bursts, undermines their ability to keep things in perspective, find a balance, and manage the associated stress. As is the case for all dopamine-related conditions, sensitive souls suffer most. While hedonistic entrepreneurs may at times be sensitive to public perceptions, those public perceptions and failures are easier for them to manage through swagger and a blustery persona and a tendency to attribute to others or to external events over which they take little responsibility.

9

THE NEW
VULGARITY

I N MY EXPERIENCE, the majority of entrepreneurs start
in the value-oriented mould. They embark on their ventures
wanting to do good in fields that interest them. They want
to make new and wondrous things, to make life easier and more
rewarding, not only for themselves but for everyone. Something
changed in entrepreneurial pursuits, however, around 2008.

Triggered in part by the Great Recession and subsequently fuelled
by developments in financial engineering and digital technology,
altruistic values have eroded in the entrepreneurial world. By the
time the pandemic hit, hedonism seemed to reign. Young start-up
founders were increasingly attracting enormous sums of venture
capital, not because they showed promise in producing something of
enduring value, but because they were determined to make money
quickly. Everyone wanted to be an entrepreneur, yet entrepreneurship

had become disconnected from the very things that once made it so compelling: building meaningful things and solving real-world problems. It had been reduced to self-indulgence.

This trend would be easily ignored if not for the fact that it has created a super-hedonistic entrepreneurial community that today's true creative spirits, our genuine innovators and guiding lights, have to live in. Entrepreneurs are no different from other people in that there is always social pressure to conform. More sensitive entrepreneurs are expected to speak and act like their more extraverted, self-confident, scene-stealing peers. Many wind up feeling, as I often do, that they no longer belong—that they may be putting their mental health at risk by trying to persevere in the midst of ever-growing narcissism and self-indulgence.

The new environment encourages founders to make lots of money, make it fast, and make it as easily as possible. Upcoming entrepreneurs want to avoid their parents' fates: decades of savings decimated in middle-age by a recession, forced to work long past retirement age in unsatisfying jobs, all thanks to the financial wizardry of Wall Street peacocks whose investments in collateralized mortgage-backed securities had hammered a systemic risk into a weak global economic system that went bust as a result. Against that experience, the notion of ensuring a lifetime of financial security by starting something and selling it for a pile of money at the first opportunity is attractive. Much of the financial media is complicit. Their obsession with profiling young profiteers reinforces the idea that money for money's sake, oversized homes, and private jets are what constitutes the good life.

The last fifteen years have seen a continual acceleration of this trend. Not even a global pandemic was enough to stop it. In 2021, amidst a year of COVID-19-induced death, more start-ups valued at over $10 billion were born than in any previous year. This was made possible by large, early investments from venture capital firms, making paper billionaires of twenty-somethings who didn't mind raising money on the basis of promise in the absence of product.

Nor was this effect limited to behemoths. According to PitchBook, a database of private capital markets fundraising, the median implied valuation for the seed- and early-stage companies funded in 2021 was $26 million, up from $16 million in 2020 and $13 million in 2016. As of February 2022, *Crunchbase's* closely followed "Unicorn Board," which tracks so-called unicorn companies (generally defined as companies that exceed a valuation of a billion dollars before they go public), counted 1,200 unicorn start-ups around the world, often with no to little meaningful revenue.

Nobody in the tech or finance media seemed to have figured out that a unicorn is a mythical creature put together by mixing parts of one animal with parts of another. In other words, a wildly imaginative, implausible creature, a delusion. In this case, a financial one. The 1,200 unicorns in February 2022 were collectively valued at more than $4 trillion—double the value of the world's unicorns at the end of 2020.

In keeping with these developments, some celebrity entrepreneurs have also been renouncing the public restraints that used to lend them credibility. They're now neck-deep in the new era of excess. In July 2021, British magnate Richard Branson was declared the winner of what media dubbed the "space race"—the pursuit of privately funded, recreational space travel—besting fellow billionaires Jeff Bezos and Elon Musk. It's a dubious honour: tens of millions of dollars were spent on a project that produced no scientific insights and broke no actual space frontier. At the time, a humanitarian disaster in Afghanistan was nearing explosion in grim anticipation of the full withdrawal of American troops; millions were dying of COVID-19-related illness around the world, and any number of catastrophes engulfed huge regions of the globe. Meanwhile, Captain Bezos, the richest person on the planet, was building the world's largest sailing yacht, a more than 400-foot long, three-masted schooner. To be fair to Elon Musk, his public statements and commitments suggest he exhibits hedonism in personal consumption and yet also expresses value-oriented impulses: notably, building a miniature submarine to rescue Thai schoolboys from a submerged cave and supporting Internet services by satellite in war-torn Ukraine. One can be both hedonistic and Stoic in entrepreneurial ambition, straddling the entrepreneurial personality divide, making for inconsistent actions that many find quizzical.

Another illustration of the hedonistic environment: mega-influencer and socialite Paris Hilton teamed up with gaming site Sandbox to open a virtual Malibu mansion. (Sandbox promotes itself as a "decentralized virtual world" where users can buy land, browse shops, and attend concerts—all virtually in the Metaverse.) Hilton's company had pocketed millions of dollars by early 2022, thanks to her young fans who bought up Paris-styled NFTs (non-fungible tokens) and avatars and paid to attend Metaverse parties with the "OG crypto queen." That's not to pick on her specifically: the examples are legion. Cash from venture capital flocks to these firms in disproportion to actual lasting value to customers; the capacity of these businesses to thrive as going concerns wanes after the celebrity fanfare wears thin.

The late literary critic Lionel Trilling, writing about Jane Austen, proposed that vulgarity has these elements: "smallness of mind, insufficiency of awareness, assertive self-esteem, the wish to devalue, especially to devalue the worth of other people." We live in an era of vulgar entrepreneurialism, rising in intensity from 2008 to 2022.

* * *

The Great Recession was also the time that the term "serial entrepreneur" gained traction in conversations and online résumés. I saw people I formerly called managers or financial advisors or attorneys now describing themselves as "serial entrepreneurs" in the mould of Steve Jobs or Elon Musk. The researchers Rasmus Hartmann, Anders Krabbe, and André Spicer have noted that the period after 2008 marked the beginning of "Veblenian Entrepreneurship," named for the American economist Thorstein Veblen: entrepreneurship that was, in their words, "pursued primarily as a form of conspicuous consumption." The period after the so-called Great Recession inspired people to chase entrepreneurial activity for what these researchers labelled social or bourgeois class reasons, in distinction to entrepreneurs whose fundamental aim was to solve problems, create things, and add lasting value to their community.

This conspicuous consumption model of entrepreneurship reached a new apex (or nadir, depending on your point of view) with two relatively recent interconnected ideas falsely labelled by the tech media as "innovations": Web3 (sometimes called Web 3.0) and NFTs.

Meta (the former Facebook) defines Web3 as "the Internet owned by the builders and users, orchestrated with tokens." A token, in this sense, is meant to convey that one owns something, a minimalist fraction of something—say, a percentage of a digital piece of virtual art. The paradigmatic Web3 company is Meta: in founder Mark Zuckerberg's imagination, Meta takes the two-dimensional world of Facebook, with its networks and photographs and direct messaging system, and torques it up to four dimensions—a fully immersive, real-time virtual world. The catch is that owning a token is owning nothing; Web3 has not commercialized anything of lasting value.

Non-fungible tokens (NFTs) go even further: they represent a version of entrepreneurialism that is intentionally disconnected from value or beneficial impact. An NFT is meant to describe an online-only virtual asset, like a ticket to a virtual conference or an avatar in a video game. Though they gained attention in the 2020s, primarily through promotions by (would-be) digital art collectors, the idea dates back to the much earlier days of the commercial Web. In the early aughts, avatar-based online conferencing championed by mega-companies such as Oracle and IBM proved to be fleeting, as demonstrated by the collapse in popularity of the online multimedia and gaming platform secondlife.com, launched in 2003. But the idea that whole aspects of our lives could be mimicked in a virtual parallel world was resurrected by Zuckerberg in 2021.

The fantastical Metaverse was supposed to be a new digital playground in which NFTs could be deployed, whether through avatar skins, online badges, or interaction among exclusive online community members. This was a Silicon Valley hoax perpetrated on the netizens of the world. The one augmented reality service that was in widespread use on Meta in 2021 was beauty filtering: apps that enable users (teenage girls were early adopters) to smooth their skin, slim their noses, and enlarge their eyes digitally. That same year, Meta had to ban some apps that encouraged extreme weight loss or plastic surgery. Frances Haugen, a whistleblower working at Meta, came forward to reveal to US congressional lawmakers that Meta had always known through its internal research that its Instagram platform is addictive: frenetically posting selfies, seeking "likes" and shares, and drawing comparisons among various physical and personality traits harms children and creates an increasingly toxic environment for teens.

The most tangible use of the Metaverse thus far, wrote technology reporter Christopher Mims in a 2022 *Wall Street Journal* article, was playing virtual golf with colleagues, an activity popular among Wall Street financiers promoting this illusory world. Even McDonald's, which filed patents for a virtual restaurant, and Nike, which wanted its brand to be a status symbol in the Metaverse, fell for this innovation parlour game. J.P. Morgan boasted that it was the first Metaverse bank, trying to broker mortgages and loans for virtual property within a virtual world. Brands like Pepsi and Taco Bell offered NFT tokens to customers.

Technologist and independent researcher Jeffrey Funk, based in Singapore, has characterized high-profile modern entrepreneurship as "innovation theatre." The venture capital funding structure that underpins it does not examine whether so-called innovations are any good, he told me, and it fails to check if there's anything real beneath the surface bluster. Other investors describe this new habit of venture capital powering certain types of business as the

"Kardashian effect"—the tendency to favour enterprises whose value is predicated on dazzle and temporary flash rather than substance. They describe this new class of entrepreneurs as "celebpreneurs."

The Metaverse and the hubbub around it were perhaps the pinnacle of innovation theatre. And like all forms of theatre, at some point, the curtain had to come down—which it did, abruptly, in 2022, due to regulatory scrutiny arising from concerns that NFTs were being used for money laundering and tax evasion, and the lack of investor protection in the Metaverse. The media outlet *Gizmodo* started keeping monthly track of NFT scams. Metaverse-related job opportunities plunged more than 80 percent from April to June 2022, as the tech titans Meta, Google, and Apple pulled the reins on investment.

That business model is inherently suspect, and should have been immediately suspect to any overseer or regulator—not to mention to all these other companies that bought into the hype. A new NFT is created, a fraudster pumps up the price, sells it, and its token, which never had any real tie to an underlying value, falls to zero. Zuckerberg had declared the Metaverse to be the future of the Internet, only to blow $10 billion in the first few months after inception. Pump it, celebrate it, dump it—that was the entrepreneurial model on meta-display in 2021.

The worship of cryptocurrency is another egregious example of this shift in the "innovation economy." Cryptocurrencies— an illusion ginned up by Satoshi Nakamoto, the pseudonymous author of a 2008 white paper describing what has now become a darling of Wall Street (its critics now call it Coin Street) and Silicon Valley—are wreaking havoc in the lives of many of the people who have invested in it. Crypto hawkers promise security and wealth, generated out of nothing more than thin air, anti-government vitriol, and wishful thinking. Recently, one digital currency platform, Stablegains, backed by the gold-plated start-up accelerator Y Combinator, advertised accounts that would hold a diversified set of cryptocurrencies supposedly pegged to the US dollar. Known as "stablecoins," these digital currencies were intended to be less volatile than other cryptocurrencies. Stablegains promised an improbable 15 percent annualized return, considerably higher than the US national average interest rate of 0.07 percent for savings accounts. On May 9, 2022, Stablegains tersely informed its customers (through Twitter, naturally) that the "depegging" of the stablecoin to the US dollar, without there having been any real peg to the US dollar to begin with, could wipe away people's deposits. Many customers lost their life savings.

I observed this flash phenomenon play itself out in other ways in the public capital markets from 2017 to 2020. For example, I saw company executives habitually "move a stock" in the market by issuing a simple news release that contained no actual news, only outlining a vision for meteoric growth. They could issue that kind of attention-getting news release even when their revenues were crumbling, and expect to see their stock prices rise as a result. Then, the retail investor class started behaving badly, too: we saw "meme-stock mania" in 2021, a new phenomenon in which retail investors poured their money into publicly traded companies that Wall Street had abandoned for dead, artificially driving up prices of those stocks, and then cashing out. Never had there been more greed on display on both Wall Street and Main Street.

Outside of press releases and meme-stock message boards, the financial and tech media started talking more about "market caps" during these years than at any time I, as an investor, could ever recall. A "market cap"—a company's share price multiplied by the number of shares issued—is what much of the modern investor class considers to be the monetary value of any publicly traded company. Yet it does not convey the full story of future value over time. Entrepreneurship, in the ideal, should be about solving actual problems in your community—and, to be clear, getting rewarded accordingly—not market caps for their own sakes.

"Once upon a time," Funk told me, "the Silicon Valley of the past made money on [goods like] semiconductors: innovative, impactful technology. Today's gibberish about AI-this and AI-that . . . that's puffery. That's a bubble, and it's a kind of innovation delusion."

* * *

We are far past the Great Recession of 2008; for the most part, national economies and private bank accounts had rebounded before the pandemic hit. Yet the cycle of one-upmanship and clout chasing kept accelerating, the displays of extreme wealth only getting more overt.

In the private, unicorn-manufacturing, venture-capital funded markets, the vulgarity was obscene in the first two years of the pandemic. Despite what you may read in the financial media, the partners at most VC-funded firms generally think short-term and small, seeking out acquisitions as their business strategy as opposed to building something. They eagerly sell out to the newly fashionable special-purpose acquisition companies, or SPACs. Supporters of SPACs argue, with intellectual agility, that the loosely regulated, go-public SPAC process allows start-ups to attract investors with bullish financial projections, despite having little or no revenue. This logic gave rise to the ascent and plummet of British electric bus maker Arrival SA. Its founder, Denis Sverdlov, predicted with much gusto that his revenue was on a trajectory to grow from zero to $14 billion in three years, which would have outpaced even Google's beginnings. Despite there being almost nothing to back its hype, Arrival SA went public through a SPAC in March 2021. Within a year, the company was slashing spending, dismissing thousands of employees, and painting what Sverdlov called "a more conservative view."

In March 2022, the *Wall Street Journal* reported on a new start-up scandal, this time involving two companies called Cerebral Inc. and Done Health, both in what I consider to be the addiction business, selling ADHD medications to adults. Patients seeking stimulants, notably, the amphetamine Adderall, prescribed usually to children suffering from ADHD, needed only to complete a thirty-minute virtual screen. Adderall is a Schedule 2 drug, meaning a highly addictive drug—like cocaine, OxyContin, and Vicodin. The companies were taking advantage of newly relaxed pharmaceutical regulations: prior to COVID-19, an in-person visit with a clinician had been required before any such scheduled substances could be prescribed; and many states were now allowing nurse practitioners to write prescriptions for controlled substances.

Silicon Valley embraced this new "greenfield" opportunity. It promised a new pool of potential adult Adderall addicts and guaranteed recurring revenues, since customers would demand refills of the addictive substance. Cerebral raised nearly $500 million of venture capital from the likes of SoftBank, the same financial backer of Adam Neumann and WeWork, and the Menlo Park–based mega-investment firm Silver Lake. US Olympic gymnast Simone Biles was hired as its spokeswoman. The company congratulated itself for making mental health services more widely available to the public and spent millions of dollars on digital ads micro-targeting new prospective addicts.

Current and former employees at Cerebral and Done report that the firms applied pressure on clinicians to prescribe the stimulants. Growth came at a torrid pace. Adderall prescriptions in the United States shot up by more than 10 percent to 41.4 million in 2021 as compared to 2020. In just a few years, Cerebral had booked annualized sales of more than $150 million.

As these so-called innovators were being exposed by reporters, video streaming audiences were being treated to a new and literal form of innovation theatre. The most popular genre in 2022 across the popular platforms Apple TV+, Hulu, and Showtime was the fallen start-up mogul: Adam Neumann of WeWork in "WeCrashed"; Travis Kalanick of Uber in "SuperPumped: The Battle for Uber"; and, of course, Elizabeth Holmes in both the series "The Dropout" and the movie "Bad Blood." The absurd, venture capital–fuelled unicorn valuation frenzy of the early Twenties coincided with the high-profile fraud trial of Holmes, the charismatic black-turtleneck-wearing Theranos founder. Among many other offenses, Holmes' unicorn-turned-bankrupt blood-testing technology firm had misled its customers—people who sought blood tests because they already felt unwell—with false diagnoses of breast cancer and HIV.

Of course, these infamous personalities are extremes of hedonism, which is why they make for great video drama. But they are nevertheless representative of the excesses of Veblenian entrepreneurship in the years after 2008. It does not excuse their often-reprehensible behaviour to note that they were enabled by a morally bankrupt entrepreneurial environment.

* * *

Business journalism reads the entrepreneurial world through two lenses: big wins and big scandals. The health of the broader entrepreneurial culture gets far less attention. It is easy to miss, for instance, that the skewed distribution of investment outcomes is intensifying. We hear about the extraordinary entrepreneurial business successes of Spotify, Airbnb, and Tesla, but not that they are rarer than ever, not that they arrive through initial public offerings on the public markets or acquisitions by investment juggernauts or larger firms taking a significant proportion of the financial spoils off the table. That leaves thousands of start-up companies in an increasingly desperate fight for funding. Many of them, despite great ideas and committed funders, buckle or show a very modest return on a huge amount of effort.

Times have changed in entrepreneurialism and invention. From 2013 to 2016 I shared an office with Craig Hudson, a dopamine scientist and entrepreneur, at the old Fitzgerald Building at the University of Toronto; our office was Sir Frederick Banting's 1920 office where he might have conceived his hypothesis and written up his historic results of the discovery of insulin, winning the Nobel

Prize for Medicine along with John MacLeod in 1923. Banting was thirty-two when he won the Nobel, the youngest Laureate ever in medicine. The environment in which he did his best work is now long gone. Large amounts of money are required to get a therapeutic agent to market. "The low-investment days of Banting and his student, Charles Best, and the rapid speed with which insulin was created, are over," said Craig. "Now it takes ten years to get therapeutics into patients. So now you need to always think, 'how are you going to get the money to make the impact?' If you're on the edge the whole time with shrinking cash flow, small mistakes become fatal."

Anand Sanwal, himself a founder and entrepreneur, is one of the few people who has documented certain aspects of the mental health of entrepreneurs seriously and in a public way. He is the CEO of a National Science Foundation–backed data company that provides intelligence about the financial health of private venture–backed companies. His firm, CB Insights, has a repository of authentic stories from founders about why their companies floundered. Most of the reasons given for a company's demise relate indirectly to mental health. Often, the company will have spent millions of dollars invested by venture capital funds—money that came with ratchet clauses that allowed the funds to recoup their money if specified milestones were not met—a high-risk situation and an enormously stressful one. The stress leads to squabbling between co-founders, fights between founders and venture firms, and fights between founders and investors. These tensions are to be expected in any business, but they are exponentially worse when runways are short and capital is impatient. Stories about start-ups start to resemble episodes of VH1's *Behind the Music* where band after promising band is undone by pressure to perform, infighting, drugs, and worse.

Another eerie feature of the new environment we seldom read about is how conservative, risk-averse venture capitalists are transferring risk to young, inexperienced entrepreneurs. VCs seldom have more than a tiny percentage of their firm's assets invested in all of their start-up portfolio companies combined. They have very high upside potential and minimal exposure to risk, and what exposure they do have they share with select high-net-worth outside partners. Meanwhile, new entrepreneurs generally sink their whole life savings—as well as savings from family and close friends—into their ventures. They are under enormous pressure to succeed, and the stakes are personal; if their ventures fizzle out, they risk not just financial collapse but life-long family grievances, emotional upheaval, and in the extreme, debilitating mental illness.

This is risk off-loading in the guise of innovation promotion, encouraging entrepreneurs to place big bets in search of instant results. Combined with the generally faster rates of innovation-seeking and accelerated economic cycles, it puts acute pressure on founders. Throw in the widespread ethos of personal gratification and quick profits, the difficulty of attracting attention and financing without gimmicks and gaudy initial results, and it's no wonder that many entrepreneurs reach for alcohol, drugs, or any other anxiety-reducing crutch they can find. The conditions of contemporary entrepreneurship are vicious.

This makes for an extremely difficult environment for values-based entrepreneurs who already put enormous pressure on themselves to achieve their goals. It is especially toxifying for the more introverted, humble, sensitive souls to whom money and power isn't that important and who care about the people around them. The disconnect between the difficult, often long-term investments values-based entrepreneurs want to make in developing their businesses and what is rewarded in the marketplace is increasing. Many entrepreneurs find it difficult to adapt, and those who try often fall into psychological trouble. Again, it is of no great consequence to innovation or to the world if ill-conceived, short-term enterprises crash and burn. But when long-term impact-driven innovations fail, when creative endeavours designed principally for global wellbeing cease to flourish due to the floundering mental health of founders, we all lose.

10

THE ELUSIVENESS
OF BALANCE

I WORRY ABOUT THE UPCOMING generation of entrepreneurs. I worry that they are not well informed or adequately prepared for the rigours of entrepreneurial life. I worry that the ridiculous frenzy surrounding contemporary entrepreneurial activity will leave them disappointed, bruised, depressed, or worse. I worry about the cost to global prosperity and the millions of jobs that will go uncreated if we don't figure this out.

From the office Craig Hudson and I shared in Toronto, we could look out at the august MaRS building. MaRS (it originally stood for "medical and related sciences," and then the acronym became the name) is Canada's largest accelerator for start-up entrepreneurs, and one of the largest start-up accelerators in North America. Watching this hub of activity, I couldn't help but reflect that despite the hundreds of millions of dollars invested in government accelerator initiatives for biotechnology and genomics, supporters of the accelerators—scientists, business advisors, and governments—were overlooking the mental health and suffering of the entrepreneurs working there. The same was true of the business school, computer science, engineering, and mathematics faculties in universities.

The evidence of distress was in plain sight. So many young students I knew were overworking. They were "crushing it," a fashionable term for trying to ace their studies while pursuing full-time side hustles. "The pressure to start something new while in school is overwhelming to fit in," one medical student told me. Their social media feeds were packed with the self-congratulatory posts of friends launching new ventures. They felt enormous pressure to make or launch *something*, and do it big and fast. They were leaving school, taking drugs, being admitted to psychiatric facilities. "Why can't their teachers see it?" I wondered.

Jeffrey Overall, an auto entrepreneur turned academic at Ontario Tech University, understood what I was seeing. He used to live it, managing his firm's supply chain overseas full-time while enrolled in an undergraduate program, business school, and then graduate school. The "grind-it-till-you-make-it" mentality, he said, is the dark side of entrepreneurship. It has become so normalized that it's considered a rite of passage: "You're killing your best entrepreneurs. The soul tires, like a boxer after the tenth round. There's only so much you can give." The pursuit of quick success and short-term goals "means you're going to harm the next generation, and the generation after that." Professors, researchers, and academic leaders don't notice the pain in front of them, said Jeffrey, unless they've suffered it themselves. Certainly, they haven't made a point of investigating it.

Balancing the demands of entrepreneurship at a young age is difficult enough without trying to gain your education at the same time. Even some of the most experienced entrepreneurs I know struggle to maintain a balance in their lives given all the competing pressures. My old office mate Craig, a psychiatrist, dopamine researcher, and mission-minded entrepreneur, is one of the few I know to have consistently achieved it. Yet even with his profound awareness of the mental health challenges of entrepreneurship, he, too, struggles to keep an even keel at times.

Entrepreneurialism runs in Craig's veins. His father and his father's father were entrepreneurs. His brother, Steve Hudson, founded Hair Club For Men (now just HairClub), which you may recall from its ubiquitous television commercials. Craig himself has had what he calls "side hustles" at four hospitals; he produces scholarship and patents at a dizzying pace. But perhaps the best way I can describe him to you is to tell you about his car.

Craig had a medical condition (since corrected) that made him close to blind in one eye. Needing to be chauffeured from one hospital to another to see his patients, he purchased the only indulgence he has ever permitted himself: a beat-up forty-year-old Cadillac Manhattan stretch limousine. He paid about $30,000 for it and had a desk installed in the back seat so he could work during long commutes and traffic snarls. It allowed him to "enjoy being in traffic and not waste precious time."

Co-founder, with his wife, Susan, of Biosential, Craig produces sleep-aid foodstuffs marketed under the trade name Zenbev. The company sells dark chocolate bars, shakes, and powders, all intended to induce sleep. While Zenbev's sales are booming today across parts of Europe, it's a side hustle for Craig. He pursues entrepreneurial ventures to make money to fund his dopamine studies into schizophrenia, bipolar disorder, and other forms of psychosis. His research is promising. Re-analyzing an old dataset of post-mortem brain specimens (while a limo passenger), he was able to confirm a scientific idea that he published in November 2021 in the *American Journal of Medical Genetics*. It showed an important connection between a genetic polymorphism and a vulnerability to neurodevelopmental disorders such as schizophrenia.

Getting Zenbev to market was a struggle of the sort familiar to any entrepreneur. As a food with health benefits rather than a regulated medicine, Zenbev could be sold in stores. After the first several years of refining the ingredients and reducing the calorie count of his dark chocolate and tryptophan-rich bars, Craig turned his attention to the challenges of sales and distribution. Initially, he convinced the truck drivers who delivered products to Chinese alternative medicine stores to also carry his sleep aids. That didn't work out, so he and Susan and their growing team of business development professionals decided to master the art of online sales.

With an investment in online advertising, Craig's sales started to improve and before long he was accessing his sales data in real time through an interface on his smartphone. He could watch orders come in from Birmingham, England, or Copenhagen, Denmark. It was exciting to see the numbers mount. "That was definitely a dopaminergic lift, and very gratifying when it worked," Craig said. "I loved seeing the sales coming in, like the colourful displays on a slot machine. Seeing the orders light up was like a dopamine rush— it was way more gratifying than sitting in booths at sales shows."

After a little while, Craig found that he wanted to look at his sales figures all the time. He became nomophobic, a new term for "no mobile phone phobia," or the fear of being without your phone, a form of separation anxiety. Craig had developed an intense behavioural addiction. He was learning that the online ad industry "thrives on a kind of variable reinforcement schedule, and what's exciting is that the spend-to-sales ratio is not linear." He became obsessed with optimizing his ads. "It's like gambling," he said, "but you need to withhold the urge to spend uncontrollably, since you need to rationally evaluate where and how your investments make sense."

"Some people's brains allow them to listen and see—but then expunge—external visual stimuli," Craig continued. "Some other people don't have that faculty. At first, I was not making good choices: it was not like I was looking at a linear regression model and making rational decisions about [my marketing]."

Once he became aware of the negative effects his obsession was having on his normally sound decision-making, to say nothing of his fractured attention span, Craig deleted the sales data from his iPhone. He paused, reflected, and made a choice to put his overactive brain in check. Now, Craig said, he's "more distant, more reflective. I can ask sensible questions and make sensible advertising choices." (It's working: his sales have been exceeding targets.)

Of course, it's not as easy as it sounds. "Just put the phone away" is the refrain of parents everywhere. The challenge is in actually doing it. That Craig, one of the most experienced, intelligent, and well-balanced people I've met, was struggling to find that equilibrium where dopamine fuels you but does not control you says everything about the chemical's power.

11

AN ALTERED
STATE OF MIND

A S THE ENTREPRENEURIAL ENVIRONMENT
has become increasingly frenetic and economically
uncertain, pressures on entrepreneurs have mounted.
That has left many, including myself, looking for new ways to cope.
Wanting novel solutions, I have been researching the growing
field of neuromodulation and the opportunity it presents for
entrepreneurs.

If you recall, the nervous system is the body's command-and-
control network, and consists of the brain, spinal cord, and the
nerves throughout the body. The basic units of this system are nerve
cells, or neurons and neurotransmitters, the chemicals that act as
messengers between one neuron and the next. Neuromodulation
simply means altering the activity of the system by delivering a
stimulus—electric, magnetic, or chemical—to some part of it

and, thus, altering the overall effect by enhancing or diminishing a specific reaction.

When my father began investigating the role of dopamine in schizophrenia treatment, nobody had an inkling that medical science would one day advance to the point of being able to accurately target specific brain pathways. Leading neurosurgeons such as William Penfield, who taught my parents when they were in medical school at McGill, demonstrated that surgical instruments could zoom in on specific brain sites and excise damaged tissue when necessary (to stop epileptic seizures, for instance), but it was unimaginable until recently that this could be done without direct access to the brain.

In the decades since my father started his work on dopamine, researchers have been studying indirect methods of altering the nervous system via electric currents (as in deep brain stimulation, or DBS) and with magnetic fields (as in transcranial magnetic stimulation, or TMS). The idea isn't to alter the nervous system's functioning for the duration of the treatment, but to use the treatment to "rewire" the brain—to change how the nervous system will respond to certain stimuli in the future.

I discussed this with psychiatrist Jeff Daskalakis, who has been working with TMS since 1988. He is now the chair of psychiatry at the University of San Diego in California. When he completed his psychiatric residency in Toronto, my mother was instrumental in getting him his first TMS machine. While an acknowledged expert in the field, even he doesn't know precisely how TMS works to alleviate depression, in the same way as no one really knows how electroconvulsive treatment (ECT), an older method, works.

What scientists do know is that the brain is "neuroplastic." It can reshape itself to a certain extent by reorganizing the connections between neurons. This means it is possible to change the habitual flow of information in specific parts of the brain by the application of magnetic forces or electrical currents.

In effect, this is how psychotherapy works. By teaching a person to respond to situations differently and to think about them differently, therapy helps a person's brain remodel itself. As that happens and new neural pathways are established, it becomes easier to think in new ways. Data suggest that neuromodulating interventions such as TMS can speed up the process of remodeling.

According to Daskalakis, the brain networks of depressed individuals are wired in such a way that negative events loom particularly large and positive experiences are minimized. In other words, depressed people see the world through dark glasses. Magnetic stimulation to the head can pinpoint the neural network responsible for this maladaptive tendency and, by temporarily changing it, lighten the shade of the lens. A person's environment then takes over: if positive events occur while a person is in treatment—during the period of rewiring—their brains can shift and become more ready to attribute salience to them and to subsequent positive events.

If nothing good happens in the person's life during the treatment period, it may be that nothing permanent will be accomplished. The efficacy of the treatment may, in the end, depend less on the treatment itself and more on environmental support during a crucial period of time. The same principle perhaps holds for all treatments for depression—psychotherapy, antidepressants,

ECT, and psychedelics. And, also, for self-modulatory techniques such as self-talk, confession and prayer, healthy living, stress reduction, even ice baths. Ice baths, it seems, have become popular in Silicon Valley. All these "therapies" including massage, aroma therapy, music and art therapy, may be attempts at rewiring, at creating new connections, redistributing salience networks. But the redistribution, should it be temporarily successful, needs to be sustained by environmental support.

Neuromodulation in its various forms is now being used to relieve pain, reverse Parkinsonian tremors, and treat depression. Both TMS and DBS (which is electrical stimulation directed at specific neural networks) are increasingly available in North America for treatment-resistant depression, and also for obsessive-compulsive disorder. By targeting parts of the brain that are involved in addiction, TMS is also being used to aid smoking cessation.

* * *

In 2021, Matthew Burke of the University of Toronto's Sunnybrook Health Sciences Centre, with his colleagues at Harvard Medical School, published a bombshell paper in the scientific journal *Nature Molecular Psychiatry*. It held startling implications for the treatment of depression using different forms of neuromodulation. The paper was a meta-analysis—a research project that synthesizes the results of numerous studies in a particular area—of 1,169 studies that had investigated the effects of TMS and DBS on depression. Burke and his colleagues winnowed those studies down to examine just those that compared the effects of a genuine neuromodulation treatment

(TMS or DBS) to a placebo treatment. What the review found was that the placebo treatments, though inert, had consistently affected the brain: not just participants' subjective experiences of depression—the placebo treatments had actually *altered* certain regions of the brain. These were, to a large extent, the same regions of the brain that were affected by true TMS or DBS treatment.

Amid all his work on dopamine, my father never thought much of antidepressants. Early in his career, he had read a scientific paper that showed that when depressed people were admitted to hospital, even when no specific treatment was provided, they improved. This was enough to convince him that antidepressants were "only" placebos.

The term "placebo" comes from the Latin, "I will please." A placebo is a kind of white lie—it's pretending to be something it's not, but for good reason. Placebos are dummy medical treatments, and have long been used in research to help determine whether the effects of a new treatment, a drug or procedure or other intervention, is genuinely beneficial. Clinical trials of new pharmaceutical agents are "double blinded." This means that neither the person receiving the "drug" nor the person evaluating its effects know whether it is, indeed, a drug or merely a placebo, an inert pill indistinguishable on the outside from the pills being evaluated. New vaccine trials use saline injections that look and feel the same as actual vaccines do going into your arm. Sham TMS procedures use fake magnetic coils that look indistinguishable from the real ones used in treatment.

Whatever their form, placebos are very useful in medical research because researchers and physicians have long known that a patient's *experience* of being treated affects the results of that treatment. The extra attention that comes with being in a trial and the expectation of relief from pain and distress by themselves can help to dissipate the pain: a demonstrable act of care can be curative all on its own. Similarly, treatment prescribed by a sympathetic, interested doctor is likely to be more effective than the same treatment by a doctor who is brusque and arrogant. This, of course, is the placebo effect. Though we consider ourselves rational beings, most of us are suggestible. Researchers have found that even the colour of a pill can have outsized positive placebo effects. In 2012, my mother and I published a literature review in the *Journal of Psychiatric Practice* on the response of patients with schizophrenia to their antipsychotic medications. We found convincing evidence of an association between the degree of rapport that patients had with their clinicians and their perception of the effectiveness of their prescribed medication. (Of course, one always has to ask about the direction of effects. It could be that a positive response to treatment made the doctor more sympathetic and a negative response made him or her more disagreeable.)

In order to convince medical regulators to approve a proposed new treatment, researchers need to show that their intervention provides greater benefit, or greater relief, than a person would get simply by virtue of the hope that comes from taking part in a clinical trial. For ethical reasons, patients are always told in advance of participation in a study that they will be given either the "real" treatment or the placebo. Scientific ethics committees nowadays never permit experiments that fool people or pretend to be evaluating one thing when they are really intended to evaluate something else. So, some of the potential magic of hopeful expectation is lost. But some remains. Neither study participants nor their evaluators know which arm of the study any of the patients are in—the active treatment arm or the placebo arm. Throughout the study, no one knows which patients who are getting better (or worse) are receiving placebo and which are receiving the active intervention.

Here is the surprise. In many trials, the patients on placebo do just about as well as the ones on active treatment. My father thought it was because the active treatment wasn't very active, which could well be the case. But some people think that it's because placebos have healing powers of their own. That is why, on occasion, physicians will prescribe what they and their patients must know to be placebos, vitamins for instance, or tonics of various sorts. A certain percentage of patients in this situation will experience real relief from their symptoms.

Why? Is it because placebos make a person hopeful and that feeling of hopefulness is what acts as a neuromodulator? As we have all experienced, strong emotions can alter what we perceive, how we think, and how motivated we are.[8]

When my father dismissed antidepressants as mere placebos, it was the antidepressants he was calling into question, not the utility of placebos, which he thought were indeed valuable. He felt that placebos offered 30 percent greater protection (he operated in percentages) against influenza than doing nothing.

---

8   There is a fairly large literature on the power of hope, mainly in the nursing literature. There are also many reports of personal experiences that appear to bear this power out.

He and I sometimes wondered whether placebos could lead to real changes in brain activity that mirrored the effects of medical treatment. Put another way: could *belief* in the efficacy of a placebo modulate your brain and ultimately reconfigure your immune system to make you more resistant to an infective agent? Very likely, I thought: I had personally learned that an overactive bladder could be treated with a "brain signaling" drug, which apparently trains your brain to ignore spurious signals coming from your bladder.

What struck me about Matthew Burke's study wasn't that the placebo effect existed; it was the astonishingly high placebo rate for neuromodulation treatment. For instance, one recent trial of transcranial magnetic stimulation that he analyzed showed a 41 percent remission rate in treatment-resistant depression. This seemed like wonderful news for patients until the investigators looked at the results in the placebo group. In that cohort, 37 percent had also entered remission. There was no statistically significant difference between the results of the treatment and the results of the placebo.

These outcomes can be interpreted in a variety of ways. You could say, pessimistically, that neuromodulation is no more effective than placebo. Neuromodulation-seeking entrepreneurs, and there are increasing numbers of them, will not want to hear this. Or you could say—which I do—that the placebo effect, the combination of expectation, hope, trust, feeling cared for, and feeling attended to, is very powerful in itself in reconfiguring your dopamine circuitry.

I was looking for a novel technique, neuromodulation, to help entrepreneurs with mental health problems but what I found, instead, was that "soft" science (psychology) treatments were as powerful as technological advances.

* * *

A pharmaceutical mental health intervention that entrepreneurs often prefer and build new business ventures around is psychedelics. In the last couple of years, entrepreneurs, venture capitalists, and hedge funds have deemed psychedelics to be among the sexiest start-up opportunities (much like cannabis a few years prior). Many also seek them out in their own lives. Psychedelics are the twenty-first century version of Aldous Huxley's "soma," the pharmaceutical answer to all life's problems in *Brave New World*. As a result, a lot of entrepreneurs have entered the psychedelics industry since 2015. It is novel, there is evolving regulatory acceptance of it, and it combines pharmaceuticals and psychotherapy, producing reportedly quasi-spiritual experiences.

There is a distinct, practical challenge to demonstrating the efficacy of psychedelics. Treatment needs to be proven to be effective through clinical trials in which, as we know, best practice demands that you expose one random group of participants to the real treatment and another to a placebo. Psychedelics, including ketamine, psilocybin, and MDMA, yield immediate, well-characterized dissociative and hallucinogenic effects—in other words, an intense dopaminergic rush. You can use an inert pill or intravenous saline solution as a placebo control in trials of most conventional drug treatments because they don't generate immediate sensory effects—patients aren't expecting to have their consciousness altered. But that won't work for testing psychedelics in a clinical trial.

As Dr. Amy Newman of the US National Institute on Drug Abuse told me, "there is no real way to do a double-blind study" with psychedelics. In one frequently cited study, conducted by Jennifer Mitchell and colleagues in the neurology department at the University of California, San Francisco, researchers ran a multi-centre trial investigating the efficacy of MDMA for treating PTSD. Published in the journal *Nature Medicine* in 2021, this study epitomizes what Matthew Burke and his colleague Daniel Blumberger of the University of Toronto's Faculty of Medicine called, in a subsequent review, "the Gordian knot of blinding and placebo effects currently faced by psychiatry." In their trial, Mitchell and her colleagues found significant improvement in PTSD symptoms of patients treated with MDMA versus those treated with a placebo. But the question, as Burke and Blumberger pointed out in their paper, is whether "their improvement [would] have exceeded the improvement of patients given an active placebo, one producing psychedelic-like sensations and thus convincing them that they were getting the real thing?"

The authors of the MDMA study defended their study design, even though they provided data showing that 81 out of 90 (or 90 percent) of participants may have guessed whether they'd received the hallucinogen or the placebo. I don't doubt, by the way, that psychedelics can, like so much else, neuromodulate neural networks. What I question is whether any lasting medical benefit can come from it; the data, as of mid-2022, are not yet convincing to me.

Meanwhile, the research is now clear that strong placebo effects *can* alter the release and regulation of neurotransmitters. We know this from considerable research, including a notable paper published in 2020 by scientists Luanna Colloca and Arthur Barsky in *The New England Journal of Medicine*. The results show that highly promoted psychedelic treatments for both physical and psychic pain can generate extremely robust placebo effects through what placebo researchers call "high therapeutic expectations."

In 2021 and 2022, business journalists and venture capitalists paid considerable attention to some small but impressive-sounding studies by Johns Hopkins Medicine researchers, showing that treatment with psilocybin relieved major depressive disorder symptoms in adults. On its website, Johns Hopkins notes that, "[f]or over 15 years the Johns Hopkins Psychedelic Research Unit has been the preeminent and most productive research team in the United States conducting human research with psychedelics. They have shown breathtaking scientific productivity, having published more than fifty peer-reviewed manuscripts on psychedelics, including fifteen published laboratory studies." What the research unit doesn't say on its website—or in its promotional TedMed talk, or in the aired *60 Minutes* profile about their work—is that the placebos used to generate the treatment versus placebo rate (the measure of success) were unable to fool the patient.

In their review of the MDMA study, Burke and Blumberger proposed alternative, more rigorous approaches to testing the efficacy of drugs. Their suggested protocols included a placebo that was not inert—that produced subjective sensations that could be considered similar to those expected from the actual therapeutic agent that is being tested. One possibility, they suggest, is the short-acting and safe hypnotic-sedative drug midazolam. It would not fool people familiar with the effects of psychedelics but might produce enough of a feeling of being in an altered state to convince drug-naïve individuals that they were receiving the active drugs.

Another option they propose is using a very low dose of the psychedelic drug that's being studied: too low to be considered therapeutic (i.e. not enough to significantly alter the brain) but still capable of producing appreciable subjective effect. These solutions may be imperfect but would be interesting to try.

A recent article in 2022 in the journal *Transcultural Psychiatry* by Gabriella Gobbi and colleagues at McGill University reminds us that psychedelics have been in use for more than 3,000 years in the context of religious healing. The suggestion is that their effects are not purely neurobiological but depend very much on the relationship you establish with the person or persons that go through your consciousness-altering journey with you. That relationship and the shared communication that comes with the treatment can be considered part of the placebo effect, but it could, from another perspective, be considered the main part of the cure.

Against this backdrop of limited clinical proof of their efficacy, psychedelics already constituted, by spring 2021, a billion-dollar industry with projections from venture capitalists and other investor groups that the global market for psychedelics could multiply to ten times that amount.

The implications of Dr. Burke's findings are profound—for clinical trial design of any kind of drug, for any kind of treatment. Dr. Burke is a neurologist by training; early in his career he worked on neuropsychological interventions, notably DBS and TMS. He wanted to believe, as any neurologist would, that these sophisticated treatments could accomplish miracles. Yet what he was confronted with was the unexpected magnitude of the placebo effect—especially, it turned out, when treatments were offered in well-known research centres. Patients coming in from the suburbs and visiting a lab at a famous hospital or university (such as Johns Hopkins or Harvard) are perhaps more susceptible to the placebo effect than a local student unimpressed by the ivy and fancy white lab coats. Respect and admiration for the institution, and the respect for the doctor, power the institution's brand and can make placebos very effective. Because Burke found that neuromodulation and placebo were almost equally effective, he told me, "it made me pivot to study placebo."

I've seen a lot of people ask if it really matters whether it's a drug or a placebo that's making me better, as long as I am better? It's a good question. Most scientists would say it does matter, that science has produced extremely effective drugs for many conditions and that these drugs can be used every day for treatment and for prevention of serious illness. A drug that can be used every day does not need to depend on a supportive environment in order to sustain its effects. While true, as we have seen earlier, potent drugs given over long periods do tend to produce adverse effects. Ideally, we should be able to modulate our own brains and also to control our own environment. That may be idealistic thinking, but the goal is worthwhile.

Entrepreneurs seek to create new products, so they are naturally drawn to new potential cures. An article from 2020 in the *American Journal of Management* titled "Turn on, Tune in, Drop in: Psychedelics, Creativity and Entrepreneurship," claims that entrepreneurs often take small doses of psychedelics to enhance their creativity. Researchers at Johns Hopkins have found that the psilocybin experience leads to an increase in openness, which they see as a vital constituent of creativity.

Steve Jobs, according to Walter Isaacson's 2011 biography, said that psychedelics could help Bill Gates, whom he saw as unimaginative. Many Silicon Valley entrepreneurs dose up today not necessarily because of mental health problems but to help them focus at work, according to an article by Will Yakowicz in 2015 for *Inc. Magazine*.

* * *

Taking the power of placebos seriously forces us, in my view, not just to question the limits of external neuromodulation (however it's done) for entrepreneurial mental health, but also to wonder whether we can find *internal* ways of transforming the ways our minds work. I am thinking, specifically, of methods that have been used by faith traditions and by philosophers.

12

THE FAITHFUL ENTREPRENEUR

A RISTOTLE WROTE THAT "uncommon devotion" to religion was a characteristic of tyrants. He was also of the view that entrepreneurship was unnatural and morally illegitimate. Two millennia later, Adam Smith, the father of modern economics, and sociologist Max Weber, both acknowledged the critical contributions of faith to economic prosperity because of the work ethic that faith supports. In his most important work, *The Protestant Ethic and the Spirit of Capitalism*, Weber critiqued the Marxist concept of dialectical materialism then gaining traction and set out to prove that the rise of capitalism inexorably parallels the moral faith-based impulse to work hard to fulfil one's worldly duties in order to merit ascent to the afterlife.

Over the centuries, philosophers and intellectual leaders have, to varying degrees, embraced religious faith on one hand, and entrepreneurship on the other, as pathways to virtue. I was raised in the Jewish tradition; I saw as a young man that there were men of God, studying day and night in the Yeshiva, and then, on the other side of the galaxy it seemed, there were men and women of business. Business and strong faith were opposites, it seemed to me then. Other religions, notably Christianity, Islam, and Hinduism, can see in entrepreneurial activity a selflessness that helps one's community. Doing business counts as doing good deeds for humanity while on Earth and paving the way to a highly desired place in the hereafter.

As I got older, I saw people of faith as harder workers, more tenacious than others, no matter the religion. I was inspired by Bob Pritchett: the co-founder of the non-denominational Faithlife Logos Bible Software and CEO for thirty years of Logos Research Systems, the world's largest maker of Bible software. He is a lifetime entrepreneur who has worked 100 hours a week for years. "I used to be one of those people who would wish that I had spent more time at the office when I'm on my deathbed," he used to tell reporters.

A recent academic paper titled "Religion as a Macro Social Force Affecting Business: Concepts, Questions, and Future Research," published in 2020 in *Business & Society* suggests that religion has been a neglected subject in business management education. The authors—Harry J. Van Buren, Jawad Syed and Raza Mir—argue that, even though the world is becoming secular, religion continues to matter in the business world. Business ethics and the social responsibility of corporations are founded on the basic principles of the world's great religions.

This does not mean that the entrepreneurs I have described as values-oriented and dopamine-sensitive and who, in general, hold values similar to those upheld by almost all religious faiths are necessarily more religious than their more hedonistic peers. Many people I know are profoundly religious while, at the same time, very materialistic. To make things more complicated, it is hard to find agreement as to what scholars mean by "religious."

Spirituality is more than submitting to parochial traditions. It is connected with the sacred, the transcendent, something outside the self. It is connected to the supernatural, the mystical, and sometimes to organized religion, although it extends beyond those borders. That is the vein I am writing in when I write about faith and entrepreneurship: not fidelity to a particular organized religion, but a certain orientation in the world—a sense of belonging to something bigger than yourself. The way members of Alcoholics Anonymous experience lower rates of recidivism if they quell dopaminergic impulses through a fervent trust in a higher being is as pertinent as being an adherent of the Protestant tradition that inspired Weber. Regardless of the particular form it takes, this sense of being part of something, and the resulting impulse to go beyond yourself to serve your community, appears to be a critical ingredient to both entrepreneurial tenacity and to overall life satisfaction.

Regardless of the definition, the question here is: do spirituality and moral values exert a beneficial effect on entrepreneurs suffering from stress and dopamine surges? Does being part of a religious community constitute a positive environmental force that sustains mental health?

"Faith often serves as a protective factor for entrepreneurs," Sherry Walling told me. She is a clinical psychologist and entrepreneurship researcher in Minneapolis, and co-author (with her tech-company founder husband, Bill Walling) of the 2018 book *The Entrepreneur's Guide to Keeping Your Shit Together: How to Run Your Business Without Letting It Run You*. Walling is a highly sought-after guest lecturer and investigator on entrepreneurial risk-taking and mental health. Long before doing a post-doctorate fellowship in psychology at Yale, she had studied at Fuller Theological Seminary in Pasadena, California. Then, as now, her clients were mostly male technology entrepreneurs. She had lost a brother to suicide, which was a major motivator for her to study the challenges facing entrepreneurial men who are risk-takers, imbued with non-linear, high-functioning types of brains that are vulnerable to dopaminergic instability. "When I think of the entrepreneur clients I work with, they manifest that dopamine openness to experience," she said. "Faith imposes guardrails for the non-linear brain."

* * *

The research on the associations between entrepreneurialism and faith, though sparse, yields important clues about entrepreneurial purpose.

In 2007, Craig Galbraith and Devon Galbraith of the Cameron School of Business, University of North Carolina Wilmington, examined religious attitudes and their impact on entrepreneurial activity and economic growth. They selected twenty-three countries, predominately Christian countries, and examined the connection between country-wide religious orientation, entrepreneurial activity, and economic growth. They found that "intrinsic" religiosity predicted entrepreneurial activity, which resulted in a country's economic growth. (They identified "intrinsic religiosity" by survey responses to three questions: How important is God in your life? Do you consider yourself a religious person? How often do you attend religious service?) These authors conclude that country-specific levels of religious beliefs were positively associated with economic success.

This, of course, does not shed light on the ability of religion or religious practice to help individual entrepreneurs withstand mental health pressures. It only suggests that, as a group, entrepreneurs tend to work harder if they identify strongly with a religious faith.

The benefits of faith do not appear to be limited to the bottom line. In a 2021 paper published in the *Journal of Small Business Economics*, economist Brigitte Hoogendoorn of the Erasmus School of Economics in Rotterdam examined eight rounds of survey data collected in thirty-two countries, from 2002 to 2016. She and her colleagues showed that entrepreneurs who are members of a religious group prioritize values related to self-transcendence over those related to self-enhancement. They see themselves as far less important than what they are trying to build. (I recall one spiritually inclined investor, when I told him I wanted to become more of a mentor than a business operator, telling me, "*Transcendence*, Neil. You have arrived at that.") Hoogendoorn's findings are fairly constant across different religious groups, and they are positively collinear: the more actively people engage in their religious faith, the more intense they are in their pursuit of entrepreneurship. Among Christians, Jews, and Muslims, entrepreneurs are more religiously active than employees.

My maternal grandfather's brother, Marek, was brought up with his ten siblings in a small town in Poland. The household was traditionally Jewish but not particularly observant. Marek became an artist and entrepreneur; he lived on the proceeds of the sales of his sculptures, bas-reliefs, and paintings. Shortly after their marriage, Marek and his young Jewish bride experienced a religious revelation. They became convinced that Jesus Christ had, indeed, been the Messiah that traditional Jews were still awaiting, and, based on that persuasion, converted to Roman Catholicism. Marek lived his faith. All his life he attended daily morning mass, and eventually his religious devotion not only created a gulf between himself and his family of origin, but attracted negative comment in artistic circles. He was not deterred. Despite inordinate stressors in his life, his faith left him serene, well-disposed toward those around him, confident, and free of doubt.

If religious fervour can bring with it the kind of serenity that persisted throughout Marek's life, then it's an important antidote to mental distress. Unfortunately, it's unlikely to work for everyone.

For people who tend toward restlessness—which is one way of defining the entrepreneurial spirit—I feel that a spiritual practice may be very valuable. Worship, whether in solitary prayer or group prayer, has been shown to modulate dopamine surges, dampen (over-)excitement, and lead to greater contentment. Meditation has also been associated with lower levels of dopamine-induced excitability, and it may be similarly helpful. Some literature appears to indicate that mystical experiences, such as the one reported by my great uncle Marek, trigger dopamine release, so mysticism may be useful for people who are depressed.

Spirituality has proven extremely helpful in the context of managing the addictions to which dopaminergic people are especially vulnerable. Alcoholics Anonymous asks its members to put their faith in a supernatural power and their methods have been shown to aid recovery, foster abstinence, decrease relapse rates, and temper the signs and symptoms of addiction. In 2021, Kevin McInerney and Ainslea Cross published a paper in the journal *Alcoholism Treatment Quarterly* called "A Phenomenological Study: Exploring the Meaning of Spirituality in Long-term Recovery in Alcoholics Anonymous," which examines how AA uses spirituality to induce recovery. Recovery in AA is framed within a broad notion of spirituality, according to McInerney and Cross, in which AA members are presented with concepts of the divine, yet encouraged to define their spiritual journey on their own terms. The study highlights the role of secular, or non-religious, forms of devotion within AA programming. They can all serve to help bolster will power so that people learn to withstand temptation.

If I'm right that entrepreneurs can become addicted to the dopamine rushes produced by their work, by their frenetic energy, and by the pace at which they operate, then models like AA, which support people with addictions self-modulate, may prove useful to managing the volatile entrepreneurial temperament.

Another approach to secular spirituality is a therapeutic practice called logotherapy, created and championed by the Holocaust survivor, psychiatrist, and philosopher Viktor Frankl. The term comes from the Greek word *logos*, which signifies "meaning." Frankl's philosophy is a form of existentialism based on the human need to find and achieve meaning in life. Frankl's ideas began to crystallize when he was a concentration camp inmate during World War II, and it became increasingly clear to him that, among his companions, those who survived starvation and mistreatment the longest were those who saw a reason and a purpose to life. Since Frankl's book, *Man's Search for Meaning*, was first published in 1946, psychologists have acknowledged the positive connection between a sense of meaning and psychological well-being. More and more, it has become standard teaching that spirituality—which, in logotherapy, includes meaning, values, and purpose—is relevant to general health.

Logotherapy, like many religions, relies heavily on the instillation of hope, which, as we saw earlier, explains the power of placebos to modulate brain networks. Hope is an important ingredient in many psychotherapies. There are several interesting techniques used in logotherapy. One is called de-reflection (the same principle is used in mindfulness therapy), which helps people shift their attention from ruminating about their troubles to viewing themselves from a distance, adopting a larger perspective on life and its potential meanings. Another is something called paradoxical intention. In one famous episode of "Seinfeld," George Constanza decides to always do the opposite of what he is inclined to do in the hope of reversing his low success rate with women and jobs. Inverting what his instincts—his dopamine circuitry—habitually nudge him to do brings George the woman of his dreams and a coveted position with the New York Yankees. This is essentially an attempt at neuromodulation. In logotherapy, doing the opposite usually takes the form of deliberately confronting your fears on the theory that backing away or avoiding something causes more distress than the thing itself.

Spiritually related psychotherapies such as logotherapy, existential therapy, mindfulness, and meditation have much to recommend them. Recent advances in neuroscience show that spiritual experiences of faithful people such as Catholic nuns or Buddhist monks, who are experts in prayer and meditation, register changes visualized on brain imaging. These practices may provide another path to remodeling the brain.

* * *

Why are so many entrepreneurs men and women of faith? Entrepreneurs need to identify and evaluate situations and seize opportunities quickly. They require imagination, a keen sense of the future, and the ability to persevere through uncertainty and failure. Faith, to people like this, is a stabilizing influence. In his book *How Science Works: The Science of Spiritualism*, a wide-ranging summary of the modern science on religious practices and spirituality, social psychologist David DeSteno writes that "[r]eligious practices and rituals weave multiple nudges into a symphony composed of prayer, synchrony, repetition, feelings, and even posture," which is a poetic way of saying that it works.

The fact that it works is not new. Religious practice has been associated with certain kinds of self-regulation, generosity, and care for millennia. But knowing a bit about how our brains work can help us unpack the underlying mechanisms by which faith or spirituality shape behaviour. People who are guided by their sense that they are part of a larger, meaning-laden world have positive associations with the concept of meaning—dopamine has made certain values salient for them. When they engage in religious practices, they are rewarded by a burst of dopamine. For a distressed entrepreneur, this can be a gift, countering the tendency to take unhealthy risks and increasing the chances of finding calm and balance in life—what my father called quietude. Amid our tumultuous world, my father did not find quietude in religion. He did find it in his laboratory. Some may find it in their gardens. Or in the concert hall. The important thing is to be open to exploring different avenues in search of quietude.

13

WHAT REALLY MATTERS

S TEVE DIVITKOS IS A Canadian entrepreneur and host of
the podcast "In the Trenches," which occasionally discusses
the high highs and low lows and the related mental health
issues that many entrepreneurs experience.

One year into his MBA at Harvard, Steve raised money to build
a "search fund" to look for a business to buy. This is a relatively new
investor business model. Steve wanted to buy a business outright
and operate it. He was looking for something of real value that
might have an impact on the world. He ultimately purchased a
family business, ran it for seven years, and sold it in 2020. But as
every entrepreneur knows, what looks like success from the outside
is never (in Steve's words) a "clean easy line." It's more of a zigzag,
a semi-random path.

Steve told me he first really wrestled with mental health as many of us did—when COVID-19 hit. All this, of course, compounded the stress that he was already under from selling his business.

Steve started trying to sell the company in 2018. Like most business owners, he was looking to sell to the *right* buyer, and that can take a while. He had still not found one by the time of pandemic lockdowns. It knocked him and his family for a loop, with his wife and daughter concomitantly suffering health problems. This compounded the stress he was already feeling in his attempt to sell his business.

Until the pandemic, said Steve, he had focused relentlessly on the goal of selling and had never considered the effect that failing to sell would have. When the lockdown hit, he felt isolated and vulnerable. He saw clearly that he was at risk of depression, anxiety, cognitive impairment, substance abuse, addiction, and delusion, among other perils.

Steve ultimately sold the business, took a year off, and started the podcast as a form of public journaling. His interviews with entrepreneurs regularly veer away from talk of mergers and acquisitions toward more personal discussions about the mental-health toll of running a small- or medium-sized business. It's not simply about shouldering one's own burden, Steve believes, but those of your employees and investors, who have their own fears and vulnerabilities.

"In my blog and my podcast, I find I am speaking to my younger self, coaching my younger self," he said. "As an entrepreneur, the main thing that you feel most every day is not culture, or pricing," he continued. "It's yourself, it's your head. There's almost this complete asymmetry between what you talk about with investors and partners and employees and what really matters." What really mattered was mental health.

The pandemic brought about a reckoning for Steve. Mine came after my father's death in 2021. Reckonings can lead to an increase in self-awareness and to explorations of new ideas and life changes.

In February 2022, I published an essay about my lifelong anxiety, my relationship with my father, and my own dopaminergic impulsivity in the *Canadian Medical Association Journal*. Feeling trepidation about disclosing my struggles, I asked Steve how others had reacted to his revelations about his mental health challenges. "I was surprised by the reaction in the most pleasant of ways," he said. "Talking about it was hard because most people would look at me and say, 'Steve, he's got it all figured out,' but it's way more common than people think. People I knew well, including my best friend growing up for decades, told me: 'I never would have guessed that you would have gone through that.' And there you go, two lifelong friends, and we didn't know we were both suffering." So it had been with me, I told Steve: my lifelong friend, the entrepreneur-physician Sean, was suffering from addictions unbeknownst to me, while I, in turn, had been periodically crippled by acute anxiety.

"When you are vulnerable," Steve said, "it gives other entrepreneurs permission to be vulnerable, too . . . It's weird, vulnerability is the quality we most admire in others, in our employees and in so many others, but it's the same quality that we least want to exhibit as entrepreneurs."

We don't want to exhibit it because we see it as a failure, and we are worried our investors and employees will, too. A few investors understand this, but most do not. An entrepreneur searching for what is called "patient capital," or investment funding that isn't in a rush to see returns (quick profits can come at the expense of long-term success), has an uphill battle. Many investors don't fully appreciate that it can take a long time to spin a business toward maturity, that it is never a straight line, and that no one feels the pressure and stress of the journey more than the entrepreneur.

Though they weren't necessarily intended this way, Steve's disclosures about his own mental health challenges have served as a kind of due diligence, letting him know which potential business partners and investors would be understanding of his personal battles—which would value the health of the entrepreneur as core to the health and vitality of the underlying business. Steve has differentiated himself in the world of private equity by being explicit with investors and the entrepreneurs in whom he invests about the importance of managing what I call the "dopamine devil"—those dopamine-influenced tricks and travails the mind can sometimes pull on the entrepreneur.

Steve is not alone in his awareness of these issues. One of his prominent investor colleagues has a policy of never taking a board seat on a company he invests in. He wants the founders he backs to be able to come to him with mental health troubles when the troubles arise—to be able to talk about whatever they need to talk about without exposing themselves to attack. It does not help an entrepreneur to be self-censoring, especially when struggling. This investor sets himself up as the person the founder feels comfortable going to when he or she is too afraid to speak openly with board members. It's an all-too-rare attitude and a sound business practice that has the added benefit of helping people avoid despair.

* * *

Dr. Arlen Myers grew up in Philadelphia where his father was a professor of pharmacy at Temple University, and also ran a drugstore in a poor, immigrant neighbourhood. Arlen's first job was selling newspapers; his second was working in his father's store, packing gelatin capsules and loading them into bottles. After training as an ear, nose, and throat physician and beginning his academic career, Arlen invented a gadget that optically detects cancer of the mouth. He soon found, as all academic entrepreneurs do, that making something of his invention required navigating the maze of university technology transfer offices.

Arlen learned two things from fellow wannabe physician-entrepreneurs. First, "every white coat thinks they have a good idea." Second, "they don't have a business, and it stays as an idea."

"Even if they do have a commercializable idea," Arlen explained, "all these physician entrepreneurs who exhibit impulsivity-control challenges and overactive brain syndrome, wouldn't know what to do to get a business venture off the ground, and nobody's going to teach you —especially when it takes, on average, seventeen years for a successful new medical invention or process to become standard practice."

This state of affairs made Arlen angry and frustrated. To help fellow physicians manage both the practical challenges of creating a business and the mental health challenges that come with being an entrepreneur, he started the Society of Physician Entrepreneurs (SoPE) in 2008. A not-for-profit, SoPE focuses on biomedical and clinical innovation and entrepreneurship. Now international in scope and considered an important hub of expertise, it is an "overnight entrepreneurial success," laughed the entrepreneurial Arlen, after ten years of plodding.

Where entrepreneurs get into trouble, Arlen told me, is in the duel between the dopaminergic centres of rewards and addiction on the one hand, and the stress response on the other. That's when vulnerable people can lose their moorings. (Arlen calls doctor entrepreneurs, "the lost tribe of medicine.") Having a genuine breakthrough—landing on an idea for an impactful innovation—can be a destabilizing experience. It's exciting, yes, but it opens up many uncertainties and calls for many decisions to be made about what to *do* with your idea, especially if you have a day job. It can, for these reasons, trigger a stress response.

A would-be entrepreneur is faced with a range of options upon conceiving an invention: fight it, flee it, or freeze (ruminate, avoid, forget). Arlen argues for the creation of an alternate pathway, an offramp from one's planned career trajectory to give the idea a chance to develop. "If you try to fight it, that makes your life miserable," he said. "If you try to run away from it, it will follow you. If you freeze it, you're left with sadness and regret. If you take an alternative pathway—re-arrange your life so that you can pursue your entrepreneurial idea—you'll be happy."

Arlen is good at counseling physician-entrepreneurs, who tend to be busy, impulsive people. They don't mind risk but they often want the reward to come quickly—which, of course, it seldom does. He encourages the doctors who consult him about their entrepreneurial ideas to work especially hard at curbing their impatience, trying different approaches until they find the one that works best for them, providing more stability as they pursue their ventures.

* * *

John Soloninka, a former mentor of mine, is an entrepreneur's entrepreneur—literally. Having built and sold several businesses, John now provides counsel to health technology innovators. (He is also a concert violinist and, thanks to his skills in engineering and music and entrepreneurialism, he remodels, refines, and resells Stradivarius violins.) John compares my concept of dopamine management for entrepreneurs to the concept of "flow," a term for a productive mental state of calm that was conceived and popularized by the Hungarian-American psychologist Mihaly Robert Csikszentmihalyi. When you look up from your desk, not having realized that hours passed as you've been working away at something—that's flow.

Csikszentmihalyi discovered, after a lifetime spent interviewing high-performance athletes, musicians, and artists—individuals who are value-oriented entrepreneurs as I understand the term—that for these people, happiness is not a stable state they achieve but an ongoing practice they cultivate. They are most creative, productive, and content when in a state of flow. During periods of stagnation, they're miserable. John told me that the people I describe as dopamine-sensitive entrepreneurs sound just like this: they "face fears that can paralyze, but also excitement that energizes."

John's father had been what John calls an eclectic polymath engineer. He "ran five companies and had five heart attacks, then ran around the world continually pursuing higher heights in business—and then he died." In the aftermath, John developed what he calls "activities of detachment that enable him to disentangle from the frenetic world of entrepreneurship."

Like all value-oriented entrepreneurs, John has suffered what appears from the outside to be failure, and what felt like torturing sadness, too. At one point, he had collected investor pledges of $500 million. He had moved his family to Barbados when he planned to repurpose certain drugs off-patent to treat a wide range of conditions. It was a business with great buzz and potential. Along came Martin Shkreli, the former hedge fund manager, now a convicted felon, whose business model raised the prices of related drugs by a factor of fifty-six. Shkreli's corrupt behaviour crushed the sector entirely, John told me, vaporizing the funding he needed to scale his early-stage company.

That sort of entrepreneurial experience can be crushing. But it wasn't John's first failure. Years earlier, he had sold one of his start-ups while retaining a position with the company. The CEO who had taken over proved intractable in many ways that were detrimental to the business. Faced with this obstinacy, John abruptly resigned without having another job lined up and forgoing earn-outs from the sale of his business. "This was very, very hard on me and everyone around me," John said. "If I were ever close to suicidal, that would have been the time."

John had defined himself as an entrepreneur. His company had been critical to that identity. Without it, he felt the need to redefine his life. And then, one day, he woke up realizing that it might not be a question of redefining but of expanding his self-definition. Like all of us, John is many things: a husband, a father, a dog and cat owner, a violinist. This new perspective was crucial to managing not only that early business distress but the collapse of his plans in Barbados.

I asked John if he felt the investor ecosystem indulges unhealthy activities in entrepreneurs who may be at risk of dopamine-fuelled impulsivity. "How many months do you have to talk about this?" he laughed. "It's a tremendously dysfunctional investor ecosystem." There is a fetish with the appearance of success that is mutually self-reinforcing, he said. "Venture capital investors gravitate toward people who *appear as successful* in the financial media, and claim that what these people exhibit and do is *best practice*. They love unbridled optimism and will often talk about how it is common to all successful entrepreneurs," he said. Of course, the appearance of success and unbridled optimism can attach just as easily to commercially unsuccessful ventures and unsuccessful entrepreneurs as successful ones. Investors will drive their founders hard to keep up the appearances and justify their optimism, indifferent to the human toll of this way of thinking. Everyone loves the story of the young entrepreneur with flash—"the bullshit that isn't real," he told me.

Also the CEO of a venture debt fund, John has reviewed hundreds of early-stage technology companies and invested in thirty-six of them. What differentiates the people whom I've called value-oriented Stoic entrepreneurs, he believes, is that even though they are especially sensitive to dopamine fluctuations, they can separate themselves as individuals from the goals that they believe are worth pursuing. He compares them to Volodymyr Zelensky of Ukraine holding the line against Putin's brutal invasion and irredentism. "President Zelensky knows that if he dies, he will have died fighting the good, honourable fight." He has a mission and a purpose outside of himself; because of that, he's less concerned about his own fate. Value-oriented entrepreneurs, too, are fuelled by something bigger than themselves and, because of that, may unfortunately neglect their personal mental health.

John has seen researchers win strings of patents for new cancer treatments that they never try to licence, because they are afraid—personally afraid. They admit to him that they fear that if the licence doesn't commercialize, they will lose their public identities as researchers with potential cures for cancer. Those self-images remain intact if they don't try to commercialize: they are still people on paths to great breakthroughs. Value-oriented entrepreneurs are different, said John. They *want* to go into the ring, seek to commercialize their ideas and create value and rewards for others; and as a result of that they risk failure and may encounter public humiliation if they do fail, which is the statistically likely outcome.

I agree with John that detachment is something that dopamine-sensitive entrepreneurs need to achieve. In my experience, they often aren't able to do so easily, but there is hope for them, beginning with a self-awareness of mortality.

* * *

For much of my life, like most people, I spent little time contemplating death. I would inevitably think about how ephemeral life can be in reaction to certain events in the news, or to obituary notices I happened to come across, or when I received word of the death of friends and family. There was one instance in Grade 5 when my teacher, Maria Pasquino, asked all the kids in our class to write what they were most afraid of. I wrote "death." Ms. Pasquino was concerned enough to call my mother. Our culture hasn't normalized thinking about death outside of specific circumstances.

Pema Chödrön's classic book *When Things Fall Apart* is drawn from traditional Buddhism. She notes that modern Western fears, humdrum day-to-day trepidations, are really all about the one true fear that grips us, the fear of death. We aren't conscious of it until circumstances force the point.

I have reflected on mortality every day since my father died in 2021. At first this was instinctual, perhaps an inevitable consequence of losing a parent. Eventually, meditating about death became a habit and, I realized, an empowering one. In my reading I picked out passages about the consolations of mortality.

"Entrepreneurs need to be fluent in grief," the psychologist and entrepreneur researcher Sherry Wallings told me. This is essential, but also taxing. "How do we keep businesses and entrepreneurs mentally healthy, especially with grief being one of the foundational factors of the Great Reshuffle of the new start-up economy?" she asks. "Why do entrepreneurs need to be fluent in grief," I asked her, but I already knew what her answers would be. Brilliant innovative ideas may prove impractical or simply fail. A business seems to be humming along, COVID-19 hits, and it sputters and dies. Spouses are devoted to your cause until they're not because you've been distant, physically and emotionally. Children thrive until they're teenagers and then they scream invective at your entrepreneurial fixations. You are juggling too many balls in the air and they all come crashing down. Your enterprise, your business in which you've invested so much, lets you down. You grieve. You mourn the business as you would a death in the family. You desperately seek consolation. That's why you need to be fluent in grief.

In the time since my father's death, in my own journey of grief, I have sought out experts in consolation, both in the pages of books and in real life as well. Thinking about the consolations of mortality in the context of entrepreneurship can offer hope to all entrepreneurs.

Michael Ignatieff, a polymath historian and a prolific writer, is well known for losing a national election, failing in his bid to become prime minister of Canada. But his legacy, I would argue, is far broader than that. An accomplished writer, Ignatieff is the author of one of the finest essays I've read about death. The last essay in his book *On Consolation* is about the late Dame Cicely Saunders, an entrepreneur who, after an illicit love affair with a patient, which made her fluent in grief, invented the concept of hospice care, a consolation not only to herself but to the millions who have benefited from end-of-life care.

Another essay in *On Consolation* is devoted to Václav Havel, the political dissident. Ignatieff writes about Havel in jail, composing long letters of love and remorse to his wife, Olga, and about Havel's distinction between optimism and hope. "Hope," Havel wrote, "is definitely not the same thing as optimism. It is not the conviction that something will turn out well, but the certainty that something makes sense, regardless of how it turns out."

This may be the value-oriented entrepreneur's credo and solace. Optimism is simplistic and often dangerous: it is often an act of wishful thinking, a form of bravado. When divorced from reality, it can result in mere innovation theatre and turn entrepreneurs into short-term "names" (not people), to be lauded, emulated, then dropped in rapid succession. Hope, as Havel says, is materially different. Having hope in the sense Havel defines it is the *certainty* that life has meaning and that the meaning *will* be found. It may not be a happy find, but it will make sense.

Havel's hope, in a way, is another term for sense-making akin to what I described, a couple of chapters ago, as finding faith. It's a form of devotion in the strict meaning of the word—a spiritual practice and contemplative observance.

Perhaps *acceptance*, then, is the state to strive toward. It is essential for those of us so easily knocked off balance by the highs and lows of dopamine fluxes.

14

RETHINKING HEALTH FOR ENTREPRENEURS

ANY OF US HAVE nurtured grandiose or paranoid thoughts at some point, imagining ourselves at the centre of scenarios in which we are either hero or victim. This may be especially true of entrepreneurs, who can easily believe that competitors or greedy investors are out to get them or, if they have a particularly good quarter and pull in unexpected revenue, that they are geniuses. Having such thoughts persistently—developing paranoid delusions and blaming others for failures or, alternatively, taking excessive credit for successes—is commonplace among entrepreneurs. It may even be inevitable and neurologically protective: it may be impossible to always remain fully rational when vigorously pursuing a business or creative venture.

For the most part, this isn't pathological (although those outside the community might find it odd). Even when these deluded thoughts reach the level of pathology, persistently preoccupying a person to the point that everyday responsibilities are neglected, it is usually temporary.

As we have seen, depression, addiction, anxiety, bipolarity, and impulsivity are routine among entrepreneurs. Though these can take a severe toll, they can be treated, mitigated, and healed by proper treatments and self-management techniques.

I am neither a physician nor a scientist; I am a student of risk and dopamine, yet not equipped to provide medical advice. And I am not suggesting that paying attention to the placebo cluster of healing methods—prayer or meditation or other contemplative practices—should supplant or exclude the cognitive therapies and the other strategies used by psychologists and psychiatrists. I do, however, think that many such interventions can be relevant. Healing can and does come from many sources, and most of us need more than one.

The constellation of sentiments I've been writing about— hope, determination, belief, inspiration, sense of purpose—sit uneasily within modern capitalism but they can, if we let them, play important roles in the lives of entrepreneurs. There have been few randomized controlled trials of the efficacy of these practice components on entrepreneurs, although there's a fairly large literature on the power of hope, mainly in the nursing literature. There are also many personal testaments to the power of hope and faith; I have found these helpful to me in my struggles, and I offer them in that same spirit.

My taxonomy of entrepreneurs—my division of innovators into hedonist and Stoic value-oriented camps—is unscientific. My father would urge me to conduct proper trials, with proper controls, to determine whether there's merit to such a categorization. My psychiatrist mother, on the other hand, would probably argue that proper trials are suitable for finding solutions applicable to large populations, but that personal narratives are the best way to understand individuals. The narratives I have included here have helped me understand myself and the growing entrepreneurial community. Perhaps they will do the same for the reader.

My father had hoped that his identification of dopamine receptors as the site of action for antipsychotic drugs might lead to the discovery of the cause of schizophrenia, and, further, help make sense of other maladies such as Parkinson's disease and bipolar disorder. So, too, did the world-leading dopamine researchers who worked with him day and night, Hubert van Tol and Chaim Niznik. Both died young. Hubert van Tol, who was born on September 20, 1959, in Maastricht, The Netherlands, died at age forty-six when hit by a truck as he was cycling to work at the Centre for Addiction and Mental Health (CAMH) in Toronto. Chaim Niznik, the son of a Montreal rabbi, died of a heart attack in his office at CAMH at age forty-three.

My father, Hubert, and Chaim did not discover the cause of schizophrenia. But they did move the dopamine field of brain neurochemistry forward. I know I won't be able to put my finger on what precisely it is that makes some scientific entrepreneurs like Hubert and Chaim chase after impact even as the chase harms them. Chaim smoked too many cigarettes as he feverishly pursued his work. Hubert was in too much of a hurry to get to the lab that morning. These weren't just men who studied the effects of dopamine; they *lived* dopamine. Neither ever stopped working, and they were both very much the kind of value-oriented entrepreneurs who are the heroes of this book. I am endlessly inspired by their work.

I am hoping this book will help people who are driven, as Hubert and Chaim were driven, to pause, to find more balance, to temper their astonishing, sometimes too-abundant energy. We can all accomplish more and run further if we slow down the pace.

* * *

Dopamine-sensitive entrepreneurs, by their very nature, are prone to experiences that characterize affective illnesses: depression, on one hand, which can manifest as being constantly hard on yourself, and mania, on the other. Does this need treatment?

This may not be as simple a question as it sounds. Making a firm diagnosis of any specific illness is a knotty problem in psychiatry. There are no validating blood tests or X-rays for psychiatric illnesses; as discussed earlier, diagnoses are made on the basis of a person's reported symptoms. What counts as a symptom, what a person experiences as unusually distressing, or what society's norms and standards deem unusual, aren't fixed. A level of stress that many people might find debilitating may be entirely normal for someone else.

To combat the stigma that has attached to mental illness through history, psychiatrists have long wanted to place these conditions on the same footing as other medical disorders. This means categorizing the various symptoms into demarcated diseases, with a biological footprint and a hypothesized genetic basis for each. That is what's called the medical model of psychiatric illness. But this may not be possible. Personal quirks are so bound up with social norms, with prevailing (and changing) standards of what is "neurotypical," that the difference between eccentricity and mental illness is never easy to delineate, especially among entrepreneurs. Is there a way we can remodel the entrepreneurial world to help us quell the pathological effects of entrepreneurial eccentricity and neuroticism? This is the question to which I turn in the final chapter of this book.

15

REMAKING THE ENTREPRENEUR'S WORLD

A N OUNCE OF PREVENTION, the quintessential entrepreneur Ben Franklin once said, is worth a pound of cure. Strikingly, this isn't something entrepreneurs talk about in the context of their own working lives. Many of our brightest and most productive entrepreneurs suffer a great deal of avoidable pain because of their sensitivity to dopamine overdrive. I believe, as I've explained in the last few chapters, that this can be controlled—that people can learn to better manage their dopamine sensitivity.

But what could be done to prevent this dynamic from emerging in the first place? If entrepreneurs have been conditioned through social expectations to operate in a perpetual state of frenzy—to find that state of mind rewarding—then what would it take to change this conditioning? Can we imagine an entrepreneurial environment that does not unduly reward short-term success and short-term bravado? One in which giving businesses time to develop and mature is the norm rather than the exception?

WHAT, IN OTHER WORDS, CAN BE DONE TO CREATE A HEALTHIER ENTREPRENEURIAL ECOSYSTEM?

Of course, we are each responsible for ourselves. There is much that individuals can and should do to stay balanced. But no matter your commitment to philosophic consolation, to spiritual fulfilment, to Stoicism, or to patience, you will still be vulnerable if the community of which you are a part rewards opposing values. Patience and self-control, as we have seen earlier in this book, are not virtues that the present investor ecosystem holds in high esteem.

What might such a health-inducing entrepreneurial system look and feel like? How can we nurture entrepreneurial wellness, promote prosperity and patience in entrepreneurship, while, at the same time, recognizing that recurrent failures, blistering curveballs and extreme risk-taking are to be expected in the business world? What can we do for values-focused founders, sensitive souls, prone to mental health fallouts created by the risks they need to take and the pressures they are constantly under?

In attempting to answer these questions, I first turned to psychiatrist Michael Freeman. As a psychiatrist to entrepreneurs, and as a serial entrepreneur himself, Dr. Freeman understands

172

the significance of entrepreneurial contributions to the world's economy first-hand. He also understands their pain. He started, as usual, with harsh truths, highlighting that the systemic problems are probably more dire than I've described. It isn't just that the entrepreneurial ecosystem is unhealthy, that it prioritizes fast, cheap returns, and that it penalizes patience and moderation. That would be bad enough, but at least we want to be able to say people knew what they were signing up for, and yet they often don't know, he told me. It's not as though these changes have happened in the shadows: everything I've said about the entrepreneurial world is well known in the community once you're in it; it just isn't discussed in an open and serious manner. New recruits are insufficiently aware of the mental health risks they will face. This next generation of innovators needs to be protected.

"The entrepreneurship industry," Freeman told me, "is notorious for glamourizing entrepreneurship, and media outlets are eager to amplify this message." There is nothing innocuous about this advertising. "By focusing on all the wondrous possibilities, the excitement, creativity, flexibility, and autonomy that accompanies business-building . . . the pre-entrepreneurs, early-stage founders, and young adults who are uncertain about the future are enticed to drink the Kool-Aid, poured without charge by accelerators, incubators, boot camps, and university-based entrepreneurship programs."

Some entrepreneurs have turned self-perpetuation into an industry. They are selling a career and a lifestyle as though it were a glitzy new product when many of the people they're trying to convince may not actually want or need to buy in. Entrepreneurship, especially in our present age, isn't for everyone, and it's a bad idea to lure people to it when they aren't equipped or suited to this very particular mode of life.

Looking at the dollars invested in accelerator and incubator programs in particular, Freeman puts the price tag on what he calls the "wildly successful entrepreneurship industry"—successful insofar as it wins acclaim and attention from governments, universities, financial media, and businesses—at more than $13 billion per year in the United States alone. This is a conservative figure that is often cited in the modern business literature, matching old 2009 numbers compiled by research from what used to be known as the "Seed Accelerator Rankings Project" (with its many reports historically posted on the no longer operative website, seedrankings.com). I suspect the annual spend on what Dr. Freeman calls the "entrepreneurship industry" to be markedly higher today, since now there are more than 2,000 accelerators and incubators across the United States, run by private and public entities seeking financial gains from equity in the so-called accelerated companies. Freeman maintains that the upshot of all this activity for entrepreneurs and would-be founders can be harmful. He points to research by Richard Hunt at Virginia Tech and Kip Kiefer at Rollins College that documents how many young founders are traumatized by their experiences as entrepreneurs and get doors slammed in their faces when they later try to get back on their feet in the working world as regular employees. The painful consequences of becoming an entrepreneur can be long-lasting: it isn't something to be entered into lightly.

Another study, published in 2021 in the *Strategic Management Journal* by entrepreneurship researchers Jeroen Mahieu, Francesca

Melillo, and Peter Thompson, focuses on Belgian entrepreneurs but is transferable to other parts of the world. These investigators wanted to better understand the now well-documented phenomenon that entrepreneurs show dramatically reduced earnings when they return to the wage sector after an entrepreneurial failure. Using administrative data, the researchers compared wages of Belgian entrepreneurs who had returned to regular work and regular Belgian employees and discovered that five years down the line, employees were out-earning the entrepreneurs by 27 percent.

The research attributed 60 percent of the earnings gap to hours worked: the ex-entrepreneurs opted to work fewer hours, presumably because they continued to try to launch new business ventures. The remaining 40 percent of the earnings gap seemed to be due to bias on the part of employers who tend to look askance at former business founders; they don't trust that they'll stay on the job. Recruiters who place senior executives into corporate jobs echo this sentiment. There are rare former founders who exited at the top and who can appear extremely attractive to prospective employers looking for a turnaround leader for their enterprise. The vast majority of founders, however, only have on their CVs what appear to human resource professionals as amateurish flings or dilettantish diversions that ended in failure.

SO, WHAT IS TO BE DONE?

Michael Freeman recommends four changes. First, the industry needs to rein in its self-promotion and communicate more realistic messages about the financial uncertainty and hardship that comes with entrepreneurship. Canadian economist Patrick Luciani agrees that this might help send the right messages and recruit the right type of entrepreneurs, moving us away from a culture that tells us anyone can be an entrepreneur. "It would not be difficult," Freeman told me, "to warn pre-entrepreneurs that most start-ups fail, that entrepreneurship involves taking on a great deal of personal risk, and that success depends upon a number of factors that are completely beyond the control of the founder, including good fortune."

Second, Freeman suggests that early entrepreneurs can be offered vocational screening before they take the plunge, to make sure that entrepreneurship is a good fit for their specific aptitudes and personalities. He points to how early career assessment and vocational testing and screening have been foundational human resource development practices ever since Frank Parsons started the Vocational Bureau of Boston in 1908 and Edward Strong launched the Strong Vocational Interest Inventory in 1927. Freeman thinks that warning mismatched candidates against entrepreneurship early on could prevent unnecessary pain and suffering down the road.

Third, Freeman argues that governments should provide unemployment insurance to entrepreneurs. Many people who hold salaried jobs have this safety net if laid off, he notes, but people who create jobs for others are often left to their own devices. According to a 2020 paper in *The Journal of Finance* by Johan Hombert and colleagues at HEC Paris, when the French government changed its unemployment insurance program to include entrepreneurs whose companies failed, it allowed these men and women to bounce back successfully. Over time, the rejuvenated entrepreneurs outpaced their start-up peers in terms of employment growth, productivity, and company survival rates.

Fourth, Freeman advocates for better mental health supports for entrepreneurs. We know from what I've outlined in this book that entrepreneurs suffer from a wide variety of mental health problems at much higher rates than the rest of society. The mental health and investor ecosystems are grossly unprepared to offer the emotional supports so desperately needed by the more vulnerable entrepreneurs.

These are compelling suggestions that deserve further discussion and investigation. Two of them are immediately convincing to me. Like Freeman, I believe that if we can help talented, forward-looking, but emotionally vulnerable entrepreneurs bounce back from their traumas, the benefits to world prosperity as well as their individual well-being will be tremendous. And I, too, want the romantic narrative that glamourizes entrepreneurship to be rewritten.

The other two proposals are trickier. Vocational screening for identifying potential entrepreneurs is difficult given that their profiles don't always fit a specific checklist of attributes or educational credentials, or fit neatly into any particular mould. Are the likes of Anthony Bourdain and Kate Spade going to pass vocational screening as we know it today? We'd need to get much better at it.

Moreover, our society has found that diversity is a good thing. Diversity of personality and of background and of experience is good for the field of entrepreneurship. Vocational screening is, in fact, based on the same cognitive error that early-stage investors make habitually; they tend to see an entrepreneur as someone who shows specific attributes or educational credentials. They look for someone who reminds them of themselves, possibly an ego ideal to which they aspire. In reality, to repeat myself because this is important, what we need is diverse personalities with, perhaps, one thing in common, the wish to better the world.

As for government financial support for entrepreneurs, it may fly well in France, where people are more accustomed to state intervention in the economy. The US has come to accept unemployment insurance, but government support, at present, is antithetical to the entrepreneur's "wild spirit." Many would reject the notion out of hand. Entrepreneurship researcher Helen Pushkarskaya at Yale insisted to me that government policy can offer very little for these very private people.

There is also a danger that an unemployment insurance model could boomerang badly if it undermines Freeman's earlier recommendation to weed out from a life of entrepreneurial activity those without the means or personality to contend with its chaos and uncertainty. That said, if done right it would have a system of checks and balances to distinguish between those with a genuine interest in and affinity for entrepreneurship and those unsuited to the life. The evidence from France that refinanced entrepreneurs get better results than their start-up peers suggests Freeman's idea merits discussion, even if it would require a grand cultural shift.

* * *

There is yet another approach to thinking through entrepreneurial health that would help considerably: one modelled explicitly on standard disease prevention and health promotion. In this context, prevention would involve helping entrepreneurs develop psychological Teflon, a resistance to getting caught up in the daily vagaries of entrepreneurial life or, to put it another way, improve their capacity to roll with the punches. The expression "roll with the punches" comes from boxing, where fighters are trained to deflect the full force of an opponent's punch. Entrepreneurship, like boxing, is a "beautiful science" and, like boxing, patience and a capacity to stay the course are huge assets.

HOW COULD WE HELP CULTIVATE THESE SKILLS?

Taking this analogy still further, athletes have coaches with whom they form deep relationships over years of training. The coaches help them set goals and develop their skills and the habits they need to realize their ambitions. Coaches also provide an external touchpoint and serve as trusted reality checks when an athlete is so focused on training that the sense of proportion is lost. Entrepreneurs, too, need someone objective—another entrepreneur, someone else who has been there, or who at least understands the pursuit—to tell us straightforwardly when we develop tunnel vision, when our perspective becomes blurred.

There's also a pragmatic dimension to all this. Coaches don't just work directly on your skills; they also help you establish and sustain a lifestyle that supports your pursuit. Coaches need their athletes to commit to a training schedule that supports physical and mental health: breathing and self-reflection exercises, healthy eating, sleep hygiene, cultivating self-awareness. Athletes aren't the only people who need habits such as these to succeed in life—we all do. And for entrepreneurs, who are particularly susceptible to dopamine highs and lows, these habits can serve as crucial forms of self-regulation, helping to mitigate the ups and downs of frenetic lives, and frenetic brains.

* * *

While the measures discussed above would help to shift entre-preneurial culture, they alone are not sufficient. Even systemic or sociological reforms, like jettisoning the entrepreneur-industrial complex, are still pitched at the level of individual entrepreneurs—at helping them make better decisions, and achieve, somehow, a better frame of mind. We also need to re-examine the nature of entrepreneurship itself.

Consider the core steps in the process of getting any new venture afloat, and how the dopamine risk and reward system kicks in at each point along the way. We know from research presented earlier in this book that the dopaminergic high is most elevated as entrepreneurs first launch their business, when they raise their first funding round and first tell their friends and family of their idea, their vision. Things get tougher after that. These entrepreneurs need to be encouraged to dodge and weave past the doubters who reject their ideas and meet the endless challenges that come with getting an enterprise off the ground. They are, at certain stages of their journey, incredibly vulnerable.

What if we could mitigate that vulnerability? One way would be to protect entrepreneurs from going too far into debt. We could limit the amount of funds, as a percentage of total share equity, that early-stage entrepreneurs are allowed to invest in their own businesses. Investors understandably want to see founders with financial "skin in the game," but that doesn't mean that their exposure can't be capped, especially in successive funding rounds and amid so-called "down rounds," when the valuation and health of the firm are struggling.

Such a protocol might also level the playing field of entrepreneurship, which currently over-rewards the extremely wealthy or those who struck it rich in an early start-up, and can therefore afford to invest heavily in subsequent ventures. A founder investment cap could limit the disproportionate snowballing effects of these advantages, and at the same time incentivize financiers to take more seriously first-time entrepreneurs who don't yet have a comparable level of wealth to get their businesses off the ground.

The level of outside investment a company is allowed to take on during early rounds of financing could be limited, too, to guarantee a super-majority (i.e. two-thirds) ownership for founders, or at least super-majority control on the board of directors. This would allow founders to retain more control of their ventures, preserving their autonomy and their will to create, make a lasting impact, and, critically, to ensure they are not pushed toward chasing short-term financial rewards. Such a constraint would also ensure that businesses pass a market survivability test early on, since outside investors, with minority investment stakes and minority control, would need to truly believe in the long-term potential of the ventures they funded.

I would also like to see us scrutinize investors themselves more carefully than we do, or, more accurately, scrutinize them for a more robust suite of characteristics. Not only should these outside investors be accredited in terms of their net worth (for example, having assets or an annual income exceeding certain thresholds designated by regulatory authorities) but also in terms of their *approach or philosophy* to investing. A demonstrated dedication to patient investing, a commitment to hold on to their investments for, say, a minimum of five years, could enable founders to identify who will support their sustainable, long-term, and intelligent growth. Similarly, entrepreneurs may also wish to know about investors' demonstrated commitment to mental health, which could be established through track records with previous founders they'd invested in or through their own business practices.

There are changes we could make to the mechanics of the investment process that would nudge investors to behave more responsibly. Early-stage investors must sign off on myriad disclosed risks when they invest in a new venture, including the possibility that their investment can go to zero in the event of the new venture's bankruptcy. What if we built mental health safeguards into this process? After all, a founder who falls prey to distress, addiction, or self-destructive behaviours will put their ventures at risk. Harvard's Carin-Isabel Knoop writes that the mental instability of entrepreneurs is increasingly understood as a fundamental risk for a business enterprise. Mental health supports could be included in investor term sheets. Inadequate supports would then pop up as a red flag, and potentially make other investors less likely to sign a term sheet that reveals a founder's mental health is not adequately protected and supported. Even making early-stage investors aware of this potential risk by including these provisos on a term sheet can alert them to what they may not know or readily admit: that they are investing in a *person*: not what Wall Street analysts call a "name" or a "horse" or a "jockey," but a living, breathing human. Such a process would, I hope, optimally match investors and founders who share the values of mental health promotion, prevention, and self-care.

One of the most discussed solutions to the entrepreneurial world's tendency to move at warp speed—it's gravitation to short-termism—is an appealingly simple one: slow the operation of the whole system down. Specifically, many expert observers have suggested that reducing the frequency of corporate earnings reports, for instance, by moving from quarterly to semi-annual or annual reporting. That would incentivize entrepreneurs to focus on long-term research and development instead of satisfying the immediate demands of the investor class. On initial review, this makes some intuitive sense: if the problem is that entrepreneurs are forced to move too quickly and are being pushed into dopaminergic overdrive, the solution could be to space out their dopamine-inducing targets farther apart.

The most influential paper on the benefits of managerial long-term thinking was published in *Harvard Business Review* in 2017 by McKinsey and Company consultants Dominic Barton, James Manyika, and Sarah Keohane Williamson. They created an index of long-termism—a metric for assessing how heavily companies weighed long-term outcomes versus immediate returns in their decision-making—and argued that long-term-oriented companies perform better. Their conclusions have been endorsed by BlackRock's Larry Fink and scholars at the American Enterprise Institute and the Brookings Institution.

The debate is not closed, however. Larry Summers, the Harvard University economist and former US Secretary of the Treasury, wrote a response to that paper, also in *Harvard Business Review*, arguing that short-termism is a slippery concept and that the jury is still out. Nevertheless, one reality of business is that short-term and long-term operational excellence are both necessary to ensure a business thrives over time. Another reality is that companies that jettison short-term benchmarks such as quarterly reporting and earnings guidance might seek to replace them with other signals of short-term success, like contract bookings data.

In any event, I feel the unit of analysis here is wrong. Observers who concentrate unduly on corporate processes and public reporting are not measuring what matters, which is the entrepreneur's mind itself. If the entrepreneur feels that she is facing overwhelming short-term pressure, then she is. It may come from quarterly reports; it may just as easily come from someplace else: a presentation announcing the next product cycle, or a competitor with an announcement of their own, or employee evaluations. There is always a lot going on in the life of an entrepreneur. There is always plenty for your dopamine system to get excited about. Dispensing with quarterly reports won't change that fundamental felt reality.

We need to change the entrepreneurial environment for all of us and we need, each of us, internally, to change our relationship to dopamine. We need to increase our capacity for self-management and decrease our reluctance to seek help. The entrepreneurial ecosystem tends to ignore its dangers, consequences be damned.

Change will require both internal work by individual entrepreneurs and an explicit commitment, in the community of entrepreneurs and those who invest in them and depend upon them, to recognize that we are all in this struggle together.

* * *

ARE YOU RICH YET?

That is the question that many founders ask one another throughout their entrepreneurial journeys. It is a supportive joke cast about among values-based entrepreneurs. You're asked it more and more frequently as your venture grows. The answer is never "yes" or "no." It is a laugh, for the question is risible and every thinking entrepreneur knows this. Unless you happen to be struck by lightning like Elon Musk or Mark Zuckerberg, you are almost certainly not exorbitantly rich. Even after, or especially after, you "exit," you may be strapped with loans made to impecunious fellow founders or to former employees or have other outstanding debts.

The trick, when this happens—after you're asked, and after you laugh—is to believe that it doesn't matter nearly as much as the world tells you it does. To know that you are a whole person, not just your company's founder or figurehead. To remember the idea that got you excited in the first place, *why* you knew it was important, and the *people* you first wanted to share it with.

And when you feel the dopamine surges rising, when your dopamine neurons start firing in rapid succession, you need to remember to breathe, and to draw on whatever helps you hang on to these memories. It may be meditation, it may be prayer, it may be hope that tomorrow is a better day. Hope and a belief in a better future is what motivates entrepreneurs in the first place. The vexations of the accelerated mind are best countered if you first achieve a state of calm, allowing hope to follow.

THE RECKONING

I N 2022, THE US Securities and Exchange Commission proposed a rule to improve the quality of disclosures from large investment funds. This was part of a broader regulatory effort to increase the transparency of private funds amid growing worries that the industry is a major source of systemic risk to the capital markets. If an activity is declared a systemic risk, it means it can cause a recession. The largest early-stage technology investment firm, SoftBank, reported a record quarterly loss of more than $23 billion after an investment spree that chief executive Masayoshi Son described as "delirious turned sour." "When we were turning out big profits, I became somewhat delirious, and looking back at myself now, I am quite embarrassed and remorseful," he told reporters.

My advice: no need for remorse, but do learn to refocus on what is real and important.

In May and June of 2022, cryptocurrencies lost approximately $1 trillion in market value; investors who got out of these investments wanted real cash—not non-fungible tokens. Focusing on what is real in business—impactful innovation, entrepreneurialism committed to enduring value—now matters more than ever.

At the same time that crypto crashed, once high-flying companies such as Peloton, Carvana, and Klarna saw their stock prices tumble swiftly in 2022. Employees were suddenly albatrosses around their fiscal necks. Recruiting retrenched. The International Monetary Fund said the world economy is headed for "stormy waters." Ray Dalio, who founded the mega-hedge fund Bridgewater Associates, projected that the economy would endure five years of negative or poor real returns.

By autumn of 2022, 80 percent of US hedge funds were down and dumping poor performers from their portfolios. Early-stage start-ups without a clear path to profitability were hardest hit, as venture capitalists started focusing attention on the best-performing companies in which they had stakes. Start-ups that had passed Series A and Series B rounds were crunched to find cash to extend their runways unless they fired large numbers of staff and accepted lower valuations than they had previously received from outside investors. Those investors' liquidity from prior investments, from their public-company holdings, were dwindling. The era of easy money, reaching its height in the 2020s, was, it suddenly appeared, over.

This moment, this great reckoning, offers a chance for rebalance and honest talk in the entrepreneurial community. There are optimistic signs. The financial media in 2022 reported on the work-life balance of employees more than ever before. It is an ideal time to talk, finally, about the mental health of both entrepreneurs and their employees. A bright side of the pain many entrepreneurs are feeling in this harsher environment is that founders and young people contemplating a life of entrepreneurialism can see the risks of unwinding a company, and suffering quick financial loss, more clearly than even during the dot-com boom and bust, when start-ups didn't require anywhere near the same level of capital.

There appears to be a growing sense of urgency around fixing the broken entrepreneurial ecosystem. I hope that leads to an admission that temporary prosperity should never again be built so heavily on the backs of accelerated but fragile minds. With the right supports and self-awareness, up-and-coming entrepreneurs will be better able to achieve their goals and make their dents in the universe, for the benefit of this generation and ones that follow.

INDEX

C
Campbell, D., 48, 49
Canadian Medical Association Journal, 153
celebpreneurs, 112
Centre for Addiction and Mental Health (CAMH), 167
CEO disease, 87
Chödrön, P., 161
chronic disease, 14
Claessens, P., 9
Claude, A., 21
Cobain, K., 88
cocaine, 84
Code of Hammurabi, 70
Colloca, L., 136
community
  entrepreneurial, 58, 63
  super-hedonistic entrepreneurial, 106
contemporary culture, 59
Covid-19, 43, 65, 115, 161
  induced death, 107
"crack" cocaine, 84
Creative Commons, 1
Cross, A., 147
Crunchbase, 107
cryptocurrencies, 112
crypto hawkers, 113
Csikszentmihalyi, M.R., 157

D
Daskalakis, J., 128, 129
DBS. *see* deep brain stimulation (DBS)
Declaration of Independence, 58
de Clérambeault's syndrome, 40
de Duve, Christian, 21

deep brain stimulation (DBS), 128, 130, 138
Delivering Happiness: A Path to Profits, Passion, and Purpose, 7
delusional beliefs, 43
delusions, 91
  ambitious, 53
  grandiose, 53
depression, 87
  manic, 31
de Sousa Mendez, Aristedes, 32
DeSteno, D., 149
Diagnostic and Statistical Manual of Mental Disorders (DSM), 90
dialectical materialism, 141
The Diary of a Young Girl, 52
distress, evidence of, 122
Divitkos, S., 151–154
dopamine, 15, 23–24, 26, 27, 34–36, 40, 85
  balance, 38
  dysregulation of, 43–44
  high levels of, 38
  imbalance or dysregulation, 38
  low levels of, 38
  receptors, 167
  release of, 84
  role in impulsivity, 37
  sensitization, 102
dopamine-dampening antipsychotic drugs, 41
dopamine-fuelled behaviour, 54
Dopamine Nation, 84
dopamine receptor
  type 2 (D2), 27, 28
  type 3 (D3), 27
  type 4 (D4), 27